Constructing Effective Criticism

How to Give, Receive, and Seek Productive and Constructive Criticism in Our Lives

Randy Garner, Ph.D.

Prescient Publishing

Published by:
Prescient Publishing
Prescient, LLC

Printed in the United States of America
First Printing: August 2010

Library of Congress Cataloging-in-Publication Data

Garner, Randy L.
    Constructing Effective Criticism: How to Give, Receive, and
    Seek Productive and Constructive Criticism in Our Lives
    p. cm.
Includes index.
ISBN: 0978-0-9774997-1-7
I. Criticism, Personal. II. Faultfinding. III. Self-help Techniques
BF637.C74 G37 2010

Library of Congress Control Number: 2010908825

Contents

Introduction: Critical Queries

What is criticism? How did the term originate and how has its meaning changed? Who criticizes? Why do we seem so eager to criticize? Is it better to give or receive criticism? How can we give, receive, and seek criticism more effectively? The goal of this book is to develop a better understanding of criticism and the dynamics of criticism-prone situations. We will explore the origins and the evolution of the term. We will work to retool our understanding of criticism and seek better ways to assess and respond to criticism. Ultimately, we will examine how criticism can be beneficial in our lives and explore ways to use criticism to our advantage.

Criticism does not have to be the 500 pound gorilla that we often make it out to be. In fact, thoughtfully offered criticism can be extraordinarily valuable in helping us to grow, recover, improve, prosper, or excel—in both our professional and personal lives. The problem we face is overcoming years of training and experience involving poorly constructed and sometimes mean-spirited criticism that cuts to the quick of our sense of self. Interestingly, the term *quick* originally meant alive, as in the quick and the dead. From this perspective, hurtfully intended criticism can have a devastating impact.

As we will see, the real lesson in dealing with *receiving* criticism is in the assessment or appraisal process. It is not so much the words that others speak, but the significance we give to those comments. We are often psychologically threatened by criticism in how it makes us feel, how it questions our competence, and how it can assail our character. In *giving* criticism to others the key is to avoid a haphazard, 'shoot-from-the-hip' approach. Instead we will examine ways that we can provide criticism in a manner that is designed not to hurt or devastate, but to emphasize the goal of helping others to do better, be better, and become more efficacious. In *seeking* criticism the real key is recognizing that this approach gives you greater control over who provides the sought-after criticism and the timing in which it occurs. Not surprisingly, we will need to rethink and redefine our thoughts on criticism.

The focus of this book is to address the usual occurrences of criticism in our daily lives—the criticism we receive and the criticism we give to others. Our purpose here is not to tackle matters that involve geopolitical conflict, criminal behavior, or actions that would involve professional diplomats or heads of state. (I once gave a lecture regarding criticism when a participant abruptly asked how this applies to the complex events involving particular world crises and terrorist-related criminal behavior.) In short, that is clearly not the motivation for this text—although many of the techniques could be applicable. Research has demonstrated that the "daily hassles" we face in life are those that can be the most vexing for us individually. These everyday events are what seem to cause us the greatest consternation in dealing with others and that is the focus of this book.

As we go through the process of considering criticism and dealing with criticism-prone environments, recognize that some of the ideas and advice on how to handle criticism may at first seem to be difficult, cumbersome, awkward, inefficient, or any of a host of other terms that we all tend to use to avoid change. In fact, managing criticism is usually *not* an efficient communication process; however, treating others with respect, regard, and effectiveness outweighs being efficient. Ask

Constructing Effective Criticism

yourself, "Do you prefer an individual who *handles* your concerns quickly and efficiently, or do you prefer a person who will treat you with courtesy and respect?" In the world of human interaction it is best to leave efficiency for dealing with *things*; when working with *people*, the desire is effectiveness.

Realize that any potential awkwardness is a natural process of any new skill development. Among the many roles I have had in life, one is as an FAA Certified Flight Instructor. This is a very challenging task—in fact, some have said that training new pilots is like trying to help someone develop a new skill—all the while they are doing things that can kill you! It is essentially teaching an earth-bound person to do something that is very unnatural, namely, flying in the air. As you can imagine, the learning process is often awkward, difficult, cumbersome, and even sometimes scary (especially for the flight instructor!)—but that is just the usual sequence of events that occurs when acquiring a new skill.

Gaining the competence that is necessary to more effectively handle critics and criticism-prone situations is no different. So expect it and embrace it; do not let it sidetrack you from your own growth and progress. Of course it may seem unnatural at first, so too did the first time you tried to ride a bike. However, the reward of being able to better manage the criticism you receive, give, and seek *far* outweighs any temporary impediments you may experience in learning a valuable skill. The psychological and emotional value of being better prepared to receive criticism with less angst and anxiety is incalculable. Giving criticism to others can actually be a gift; it allows you the privilege of becoming a more respected and effective person in their lives.

Finally, because readers may choose to review the chapters in an order different than the sequence presented, there is an intentional slight repetition of some information to ensure the reader is not faced with deciphering a term or acronym outlined earlier in the book. Although the presentation of the chapters is designed to provide a logical flow and progression, some readers may benefit from moving directly to a chapter or section that interests them the most.

Now, let's improve our ability at Constructing Criticism!

Chapter 1
What is Criticism?

"Honest criticism is hard to take, especially from a relative, a friend, an acquaintance, or a stranger."
~ F. P. Jones

The Usual Definitions

What do you think of when you hear the word criticism? Criticism is a term that almost immediately evokes a sense of apprehension. Our reaction to criticism is often evident in a general perception of discomfort. Criticism is usually unsolicited, often unwanted, and frequently unwelcome. However, criticism is a daily occurrence for most of us. As a result, we can either remain painfully affected by it or we can seek new ways to handle criticism-prone environments.

The dictionary typically defines "criticism" as that which stresses fault or focuses on blame. The *Encarta Dictionary's* first two entries are:

1. Act of criticizing: a spoken or written opinion or judgment of what is wrong or bad about somebody or something.

2. Disapproval: spoken or written opinions that point out one or more faults of somebody or something.

Notice there is nothing positive, uplifting, or encouraging about these definitions; they are exclusively negative in tone and focus on "what is wrong or bad." Reviewing entries related to the term criticism in a thesaurus is equally pessimistic and involves words such as censure, disapproval, disparagement, condemnation, and denigration. In fact the antonym listed is "praise." So our common understanding of the word criticism is decidedly negative and condemning. Interestingly, the origin of the term was much different.

History of the Term

Many words in common usage have an origin quite different from their meaning today. For example *grotesque* was a term originally describing the intricate art work on the cathedrals and grottos of the historical period. However, over time this *grotto-esque* style became out of fashion and the term is now synonymous with something vile or repulsive—far from its original artistic meaning. Likewise the term *trivial*, now associated with something unimportant, insignificant, or inconsequential, is derived from the Latin root *triviem* (literally "three ways") which originally referred to the three mandatory core courses (thus important for all) required at early colleges and universities. However, as all students were required to attend these classes (grammar, rhetoric, and logic), they became synonymous with the activities of *beginning* students and were seemingly much less consequential than their advanced studies (the *quadrivium*: arithmetic, geometry, music, and astronomy). So the important *triviem* became *trivial* by contrast and the later word evolution stuck.

In a similar way the term criticism had a much different origin than the usage we ascribe to it today. The word criticism was derived from the Latin *"criticus"* (critic), which was in turn a derivative of the Greek word *"kritikos"* and was likely coined during the time of Aristotle and Plato. The term originally was identified with classic philosophers and described a way of thinking about culture and poetry. The word was defined in the context of an intellectual activity and indicated that one was "able to judge or discern." The focus of criticism during this period was to discuss how closely a song or poem, for example, actually captured the essence of that which it described. Aristotle used the term *kritikos* to identify individuals who by virtue of their education and special ability could properly appraise the *kalon* (Greek for beauty or beautiful) in poetry.[1] It did not have the overwhelming negative connotation that it has today. In fact, criticism of that period concentrated on an admiration for works that affected an emotional and thoughtful response from the audience.

"By criticism, as it was first instituted by Aristotle, was meant a standard of judging well." ~ John Dryden

---

Criticism Reconsidered: From Snipe to G.R.I.P.E.

Rather than the negatively steeped definition that seems to have evolved, let's consider redefining the term with a greater focus both on its original intent and with more of an eye toward providing helpful or productive feedback. Sniping, an attack in speech or writing, characterizes what we tend to do most in criticism-prone situation. If we move away from the pejorative *sniping*, we can see that productive and constructive criticism can be a form of useful communication that provides information others can use to better themselves. Instead of focusing on acerbic assaults, what if we retool our intent and understanding of criticism to provide useful information that helps another to Grow, Recover, Improve, Prosper, or Excel (G.R.I.P.E.)? Unlike most of our present day impressions of the term, criticism *can* be productive and constructive; it need not always be associated with harshness and blame. Interestingly, the Hebrew word for criticism, *toch'acha*, is from the same word meaning "proof." As a result, it can be suggested that the best way to criticize another is not through a harsh rebuke or condemnation, but by offering clear and obvious proof so that the person can see for themselves the potential for improvement. The goal of criticism, therefore, should be to help others grow, recover, improve, prosper, or excel, a somewhat different approach than is often practiced today.

Redefining Criticism

Although the term criticism has a decidedly negative connotation in today's world, we now recognize that the origins of the word had a somewhat different nuance. As a result, we can get back to the ancestry (literally) of criticism and forge a definition that unites the less pessimistic origin of the word with a more beneficial intent.

Considering the origins and intentions of criticism we can now offer a new definition of criticism that will be used throughout this book:

Criticism – offering productive and constructive information intended to help others grow, recover, improve, prosper, or excel.

Of course, this definition may seem to have greater utility for the provider of criticism than for the one who is receiving its sting from a critic with no such understanding of criticism's historic or helpful pedigree. However, simply redefining a term is clearly not sufficient; you can put new paint on an old barn...but you still have an old barn. We have to rethink our understanding and reconsider our goals and desired outcomes. We need to "construct" a new barn. If we reevaluate our thoughts on criticism we can find value in receiving critical comments from others, even when not well delivered. Properly assessed, it may help us learn more about ourselves, the situation, or the critic. Even mean-spirited destructive criticism allows us to learn *something* about the character of the critic and gives us an opportunity to practice our ability to keep our emotions in check.

G.R.I.P.E. in Action

The acronym G.R.I.P.E. can help us to be mindful of the productive intent that our criticism should carry. Our new definition of criticism allows us to view it as a tool designed to help others to:

Grow – Find ways to help others grow as individuals, as colleagues, or in whatever role they may be struggling with. Growth occurs when there is care and attention to the garden. Personal and profession-al growth is essential and our criticism should nour-ish, not diminish, that growth potential.

Recover – Some people are dealing with a loss of pur-pose, esteem, direction, or even a loss of respect. The idea of recovery conjures the image of recuperation, helping another to heal or get better. Our criticism should be directed toward helping others overcome their sense of loss and stem any further deterioration.

Improve – Criticism should always be designed to help another improve, whether it is at work, home, or elsewhere. The problem with most criticism is that it focuses on what another may have done wrong, not on ways to improve and do better. This is similar to the difficulty encountered when ad-ministering punishment. Frequently punishment is dispensed to extinguish a negative behavior; unfor-tunately, there is little information communicated about what or how to do things differently. Without guidance for improvement, even well-intentioned criticism is less effective.

Prosper – Criticism can be offered in such a way that it can help another to thrive. The ultimate goal of productive and constructive criticism is to help oth-ers succeed. Individuals can prosper from any num-ber of things including experience, wisdom, and, yes, even criticism. Properly considered criticism may al-low another to flourish.

Excel – Effective criticism not only offers guidance for others to improve and prosper, but to become truly exceptional as well. The interaction of a helping spirit and a willing recipient may allow another to ultimately become the absolute best they can.

So we want to reconsider our ideas about criticism and move our objective from "snipe" to G.R.I.P.E. When offering criticism to others we want to provide information that helps them to become better. The use of the term *information* in our new definition of criticism is deliberate. As we will see in later chapters, when one properly assesses criticism and views it more as information or data rather than an assault to their self-worth, the ability to *manage* the criticism is less difficult.

The Bother of Criticism

As discussed in the next two chapters, criticism tends to confront our self-esteem—the way we feel and think about ourselves. Criticism, as we have usually experienced it, often has a decidedly negative connotation. We have an almost automatic emotional response when we interpret that someone is criticizing us; however, recognizing that we do *interpret* criticism is the key to becoming more effective at criticism management. It is how we retool our thinking about the way we appraise and assess criticism that is essential for our success. Giving criticism can be equally difficult as it can often involve conflict, stress, and giving people information that they may prefer not to hear. In fact, a recent study found that midlevel managers perceived themselves to be in the "middle of the hour glass" when it comes to dealing with criticism—receiving pressure from both ends.[2] These managers indicated that not only did they receive criticism from their bosses, the public, and so forth, they were also required to deliver criticism to those they supervise. Giving criticism can reminds us that we cannot always be the "nice guy."

We cannot avoid criticism as it is all around us; we deal with it at the workplace, we deal with it at home, we deal with it in almost all settings. Studies have shown that criticism can be more difficult for us to handle because we have not designed an approach or method to deal with criticism; we allow it to haphazardly impact us.[3] As a result, we are really left with two basic choices. We can either learn strategies and tactics to become better at handling criticism or we can choose to limp along in a disorganized and unproductive manner. The goal here, of course, is to recognize that criticism is a potentially powerful force and we want to find ways to harness that energy to become better at giving, receiving, and seeking criticism in our life.

Criticism: Appraisal, Assessment, Interpretation

The late Albert Ellis, the father of Rational Emotive Behavior Therapy, long ago reminded us that what tends to cause us to have an emotional reaction to an event is not so much the event itself, but the meaning we attach to it. According to Dr. Ellis, it is how we appraise events such as criticism that can cause an unproductive emotional response. So it is not the words of criticism that causes us to experience discomfort, it is how we *interpret* the criticism. Unfortunately, we sometimes give too much power to the critic, allowing them to assail our self-esteem without fully assessing the validity or credibility of the criticism. We allow the words of others to bypass our cognitive appraisal process and permit the criticism to elicit an adverse emotional reaction. Once we realize that we have the ability to manage, evaluate, and appraise the criticism more effectively, the undesirable impact of criticism can be diminished.

> ### *"People are not disturbed by things, but by the view they take of them."* ~ Epictetus

I have often used the example of being in class when someone walks in and begins to speak seemingly beautiful and passionate French. I am enthralled with the beauty of the language and, even though I do not speak French, I enjoy listening to this "language of love." Of course, things are not as they may seem. In reality, this person is actually cursing me and my ancestry for some apparent misdeed that has been falsely attributed to me. Even though this person is clearly offering strong, if not misguided, criticism—that was not the message I received. I did not assign a negative connotation to the seemingly "beautiful French." From the critic's perspective the criticism was there; however, my positive assessment of the information prevented the message from eliciting an adverse emotional reaction. (Of course, the fact that I didn't speak the language and didn't really understand what was being said was a teeny little factor.) Nevertheless, this demonstrates the potency of our appraisal process. Even in the more likely scenarios in which the criticism is understood, we still maintain the ability to assess the information and consider our response. The appraisal process does not have to follow some automatic cognitive functioning that elicits anxiety, fear, apprehension, or angst, merely because someone elects to offer us criticism.

Not unlike the thoughts of William Shakespeare who wrote in *Hamlet*, "for there is nothing either good or bad, thinking makes it so," we too can work to alter our thinking about criticism. We can retool our view of criticism; we can redefine criticism to represent a potentially positive and productive force; and we can examine ways in which we can become better at giving, receiving, and ultimately seeking criticism in our lives. We can become more cognizant of how we all tend to appraise criticism differently. We can work to recognize better ways to assess or appraise an event or circumstance, so as not to automatically react to a critical stimulus. When offering criticism to others, we have to thoughtfully consider our true motives and goals. Why are we criticizing? What do we truly want as an outcome? Effective criticism requires *accountability* on the part of the critic for the way the information is communicated. Becoming more adept at criticism management is not necessarily easy or efficient, but it is a much more helpful and productive way to consider handling the varied social interactions we experience each day.

Chapter 2
Critical Discourse

"It is infinitely easier to criticize than to create."
~ John McCormick

Why Do People Criticize?

Some criticize because it is their job, like a coach, a teacher, a boss, or a parent. Some may simply enjoy irritating others. Criticism may flow because of something you did or said that is at odds with the way the critic sees the world. Still others may criticize for reasons that have nothing directly to do with you; they may be upset, emotional, exhausted, or they may be trying to prove that they are more important or more intelligent. They may be trying to inflate their own self-worth, self-esteem, or self-importance. Criticism may be manifested by a lack of trust, lack of knowledge, or fear.

Criticism often occurs when: 1) we make a mistake, 2) someone *thinks* we made a mistake, or 3) someone uses the complaint as an opportunity to express problems that may be unrelated to the criticism—such as criticizing your work, when in reality they are more concerned with something else. (For example, someone offers criticism about a report that you authored, but it is really based on your manner of dress or their perception that you ignored them at some prior time.) Despite attempts to offer a redefinition of the term, most criticism is negative in tone and delivery, partly because we have been "taught" that is the proper approach to criticism, and partly because it is just easier to call attention to faults. Many years ago I attended a misguided supervisory in-service training event in which the topic of criticism and feedback was discussed. The instructor's expressed views on the subject were wholly punitive. In his view, if the recipient of the criticism wasn't emotionally distraught or crying when you were done, "you weren't doing it right."

Additionally, people tend to label negative comments as criticism, whereas information that is perceived by the recipient to be helpful may be labeled as "feedback." Interestingly the antonym of criticism is "praise," further confirming the negative connotation. Of course, terms like advice, criticism, feedback, evaluation, opinion, pointers, reactions, suggestions, and so forth have sometimes been used interchangeably; however, one of the goals of this book is to create a different mindset regarding our conception of criticism. Criticism is the term that has the strongest emotional reaction and, thus, is the term that needs the greatest consideration. Although some might choose to label criticism as something else, it is likely far better to deal with the emotions, reactions, attitudes, and difficulties that have come to be associated with the term rather than to engage in a "shell game" of musical labeling. In other words, criticism is the hot button issue and the word that evokes the most sentiment, so let's deal with it directly. Ultimately, it really does not matter what *you* call criticism, as this is determined by the interpretation and assessment of the recipient. Typically, few people approach another and say "I want to criticize you!" or "I want to give you some criticism." However, people will often use other terms such as "I want to give you a little feedback" or "Let me offer some advice." Of course, what is most meaningful is how the information is considered, developed, and delivered. You may use the term "feedback" or "advice," but depending on the psychological assessment of the recipient they may still "hear" criticism.

Moreover, the goal is to reconsider *criticism* to be more reflective of its less pessimistic origin. With skill and practice, we will be able to offer criticism more effectively, accept criticism more readily, and even cultivate a desire to request criticism from others. Criticism need not always be steeped in negativity; effectively communicating criticism to others in a manner that helps them to grow, recover, improve, prosper, or excel (G.R.I.P.E.) can be a transformational experience. Learning to provide criticism to others so that they can make something better out of themselves is a gift. It allows you to become someone who is a positive, encouraging, and affirming force in the life of another—and that may be the most important contribution we can make in *our* lives.

Who Criticizes?

In a word: Everyone! It has been suggested that offering criticism is practically a national pastime—whether the critic is well informed about an issue or not. Offering unsolicited criticism is often easy—especially when one is not overly concerned with the accuracy of their judgment or the quality of their comments. Critics come in all shapes, sizes, and varieties. Some criticize as a result of their position (Boss, Supervisor), their relationship (Parent, Grandparent), or their role (Teacher, Coach). As we all tend to engage in criticism, for our purposes the real question is who criticizes *well*? Caustic criticism is easy; what is much more difficult is to offer appropriate criticism that is well thought out, well crafted, well organized, and has the recipient's best interests in mind. Truly effective and productive criticism is delivered from the *heart* as well as the mind.

Types of Criticism

Generally criticism comes in two broad varieties, constructive and destructive. *Constructive* criticism is based on more accurate perceptions of circumstances or behavior and the conveyer is motivated by a sincere desire to help the recipient improve. In fact the definition of constructive is "something that is carefully considered and meant to be helpful." Constructive criticism is offered with the goal of helping the recipient to G.R.I.P.E. The aim is neither to belittle the one criticized nor to inflate the ego of the critic; instead it is offered in a spirit of assistance. Constructive criticism provides useful feedback that the recipient can use to make corrections or improvements; it offers a suggestion or plan for change.

Constructive criticism can often be identified by the recipient because:

- It is problem-focused, not personal
- It focus on facts, not unsupported conclusions
- It is specific, not vague
- It describes, rather than evoking judgment and blame
- It is often provided with regard to helping the recipient improve
- The recipient may have heard the same information from others (adds information)
- The critic has credibility in dealing with the subject under scrutiny (adds value)

"Better the criticism of a friend than the kiss of an enemy." ~ *Proverb*

Alternatively, *destructive* criticism is not necessarily based on accurate perceptions and the conveyer of the criticism may have ulterior motives in giving the criticism. Perhaps their goal is to make you look bad, unduly influence your course of action for their own benefit, or to make themselves appear better, smarter, or more powerful than you. In short, the goal is not improvement or helping, but to injure another's self-esteem. Destructive criticism may be given to show "who's the boss," or belittle the other person. Frequently destructive criticism is overly critical, often overly general, and devoid of a clear suggestion or remedy that would help the recipient to improve. Destructive criticism may have accuracy; however, its adverse intent often nullifies the benefit that might have otherwise been derived by the recipient.

Destructive criticism can be identified by the recipient because:
- It is often personally focused
- It focuses on conclusions rather than facts
- It is overly general or vague
- It focuses on judgment and blame
- It is offered without the best interests of the recipient in mind
- The critic has little or no credibility in dealing with the subject under scrutiny

---

"It is much easier to be critical than to be correct." ~ *Disraeli*

Critical Response
Ultimately the greater concern for the recipient of criticism is not the type of criticism offered or the intent of the critic (although that is very important in the assessment process), but it is the way in which one chooses to *respond* to the criticism. This book will offer advice to

help deal with that issue. Generally, there are at least four broad ways in which people may choose to respond to criticism:

- We can **H.I.D.E.** from the criticism: Hide, Ignore, Dodge, or Evade.
- We can **R.O.A.R.** as the result of the criticism: Retaliate, Offend, Attack, or seek Revenge. This is essentially a counter-offensive designed to strike back or get even.
- We can try to **B.E.A.T.** the criticism: Bear it, Endure it, Abide it, and Take it, even if mean spirited, inaccurate, or completely erroneous. However, this approach usually results in resentment, hurt feelings, and an attitude of defeat.

Or

- We can **L.E.A.R.N.** (Listen, Evaluate, Acknowledge, Respond, Navigate) to more effectively deal with criticism by remaining calm, assessing the merits, and skillfully responding.

Of course, not all responses are equally productive or effective.

1. Hiding, ignoring, dodging, or evading criticism may work for a while, but it will not solve the problem that brought you to the attention of the critic and the stress of this unresolved problem can take a physical and psychological toll.

2. Counter-offensives involving retaliating, offending, attacking or seeking revenge typically increase the conflict. There is very little that could be identified as productive, if you are simply reacting to preserve your bruised ego. Even if you are right and the criticism is way off base, counter-attacking is hardly the best course of action. It is doubtful that a critic

Critical Discourse

will respond well to a further escalation and the situation will likely deteriorate.

3. Bearing, enduring, abiding it, or taking criticism unquestioningly, ultimately, does nothing to protect your self-esteem, especially if it is inaccurate. It may lead us to feel hurt, worthless, or defeated. Unquestioned acceptance of the criticism of others is not the solution. In fact, failing to properly assess criticism really demonstrates a lack of emotional and psychological maturity. If done enough times, the critic may come to see you as an easy target on whom to vent their frustration.

4. Learning to more effectively deal with criticism is clearly the option of choice. It has the best outcome potential for your self-esteem and your personal growth. Managing the critic is not always easy, but it is likely the most effective approach. You must try to assess where the person is coming from, determine the motivation for the criticism, try to understand the critic and the criticism, and work to respond in your own measured and reflective way; not getting caught up in the potentially caustic cycle of the critic.

As with many things in life, your decision on how to respond is ultimately your choice. It takes skill and discipline to achieve the most productive choice, but that is what will best serve you in the long run. If you choose to get in the gutter and go toe-to-toe with the unskilled critic, you are also choosing the quality (or lack thereof) of the result. Effectively dealing with the criticism of others is complex. However, with practice you will be able to better assess the critics' comments without the emotional baggage and pitfalls that belie most in these circumstances. Remember that character is not forged in the face of adversity, it is revealed.

"As iron sharpens iron, so one man sharpens another." ~ *Proverbs (27:17)*

Benefits of Criticism

Although it may not seem so at the time, criticism can be valuable despite the initial discomfort that it may cause. In fact, a number of studies have demonstrated that people actually *want* criticism; they want to know what they do well, what they need to improve, and what others believe their strengths and weaknesses are. Most people expect their bosses and others in certain positions to provide criticism. If the criticism is accurate and you are capable of change, it can serve to motivate you to grow, recover, improve, prosper, and excel. Though many critics are not as skilled at delivering criticism as we would like, we cannot discount their message. Amid the seeming assault to our self-esteem there may lay a kernel of truth that can allow us to better ourselves. Similar to the roughness of a whetstone that is used to sharpen a dulling knife, the roughness of criticism can be used to sharpen our own skills and abilities, allowing us to become a more effective individual.

A number of studies have demonstrated that those who are most successful in their professional and personal lives develop the ability to effectively handle criticism—constructive or not. In fact, in a research study that I completed a few years ago that involved over 1,000 policing executives, I found that the capacity to handle criticism was inextricably linked to success and longevity in their career.[4] Policing is one of those criticism-prone occupations that tend to attract critics from all areas. Moreover, as a figurehead, the chief executive of a law enforcement agency is often the most visible and, therefore, receives the most criticism. This study suggested that it was not the criticism per se that was most important, it was the ability of the executive to appraise and manage the criticism that resulted in a successful tenure.

Similar results were found in a study I conducted involving members of the clergy.[5] Those in the ministry are in a difficult and unique position. The demands of the position can be psychologically and physiologically exhausting. The clergy in the study reported that criticism was a significant stressor and resulted in numerous adverse consequences including burnout, health problems, interpersonal conflict, and premature departure from the ministry. Those who were better equipped to handle criticism fared far better in both their personal and professional lives.

People consistently report that what distresses them most about criticism is that they feel as though they have no control over the criticism or the critic and feel somewhat vulnerable to the person giving it. However, as we will see in later chapters, the recipient may actually have greater control in managing criticism than they may first realize. When we think about the criticism differently, when we assess the criticism and look at it more as *information*, we can begin to regain a sense of control. The criticism is viewed more as data that we can analyze rather than a frontal assault to our esteem. We can evaluate and appraise the criticism, gain clarification if needed, and determine how we might best address it.

Criticism can provide positive and productive motivation for change. Athletes benefit from the criticism of their coaches and children benefit from the productive and constructive criticism of their parents, teachers, and others. The benefits of criticism are realized most when the recipient recognizes and interprets that the comments are not rooted in malice or spite, but are directed at helping them perform better. When the recipient is confident that you have their best interest in mind, the criticism is more positively received.

Although the absence of criticism may seem appealing on the surface, it often indicates a lack of regard or concern by those around you—this can be especially true in the workplace. If you are considered by others to be ineffectual or not worth the effort, you may not receive the benefit of productive criticism.

Chapter 3
Criticism: Is it Better to Give than Receive?

"To profit from good advice requires more wisdom than to give it."
~ John Churton Collins

Criticism is unavoidable—there is no behavior that everyone will accept and undisciplined criticism is often easy to dish out. It is unlikely anyone could prevail in a challenge to identify a behavior that could not be criticized by *someone*. I have been studying criticism for nearly 30 years and I've not found anything as yet that could not be criticized.

For some, dispensing caustic criticism—often under the guise of "help"—seems to be their mission in life. Often those who say they want to be "brutally honest," tend to focus more on the *brutal* rather than the honest. The chronic critic can *always* find a way that something could have been done differently or better, some greater goal that we should have been striving to achieve, or some quality opportunity that we foolishly missed. The chronic critic can be a challenge; however, your best tactic is to recognize that their constant complaining and fault finding really says more about them than about you. Addressing the psychological make-up of chronic critics is well beyond the purview of this book; however, suffice it to say that they seldom turn the mirror of self-assessment toward themselves as the result would be psychologically disastrous.

"Nobody wants constructive criticism. It's all we can do to put up with constructive praise." ~ M McLaughlin

---

The Give and Take of Criticism
Criticism is a multifaceted subject. We often seem to be bent on dispensing it without careful consideration, yet we recognize that criticism is often not well received by others. We don't mind dishing it out, but we are not fond of receiving it. A number of studies have examined some of the issues surrounding our mind-set regarding giving and receiving criticism; some of these findings from an organizational survey are summarized below:[1]

Why does *receiving* criticism bother us?
- It's always been portrayed as negative
- It assaults our self-esteem
- It can leave us feeling confused
- It may be unfair
- It may present a view with which we do not agree or perceive
- The critic seems to enjoy the delivery
- It hurts our feelings
- It makes us seem less than we see ourselves

Why does *giving* criticism cause us concern?
- Because we know the other will likely not take it well

- It requires us to be less-than-friendly
- The critic can feel tension, even more than the recipient
- Because people will disagree with us
- The confrontation is unpleasant
- It's giving people news they may prefer not to hear

Notice that these statements, not unsurprisingly, focus on the negative. Whether receiving or giving criticism our overwhelming interpretation is that it usually has to be a negative event. Other research has looked more carefully at the psychological implications of criticism.[2]

- **Criticism can challenge our competency** – When criticized we may see this as a threat to our competence and ability. Criticism can cause us to question if we are capable of performing a role, task, or skill. We may believe we are doing well, and then we are hit with criticism that can shake our view of our abilities.

- **Criticism can impact our self-esteem** – When criticized, the way we view ourselves can be impacted. Our confidence, our sense of self-worth, or our self-respect can be affected. When this happens self-doubt can be the result.

- **Criticism can question our character** – Criticism can be seen as impugning our character. When someone criticizes our ethical or moral integrity it can challenge our very understanding of who we are and what we stand for.

- **Criticism can threaten our reputation** – Criticism can affect our relationships with others. When criticism impacts our reputation it can challenge our reliability, our honesty, and our interpersonal interactions. In fact, in a study I conducted with a group of organizational leaders, this issue was one that many individuals indicated inflicts the most harm.[3] It is one thing to criticize me personally; it is much different when that criticism, especially if unwarranted, becomes public. When this happens you may not be in a position to defend yourself or to offer a more complete picture or understanding. As a result, you are concerned that others will believe the criticism without regard for facts, explanations, or alternative considerations. It is not the criticism that is personally delivered to you that is the biggest problem; it is your trepidation about what others will think about you if they hear this criticism.

- **Criticism can cause us to retreat** – Criticism can result in both physical and psychological withdrawal. When criticized we may feel a sense of despair or hopelessness that may cause us to flee rather than dealing with the stress of the fight. We may chose to remove ourselves from the environment or circumstance that elicited the criticism or we may psychologically "flee" by shutting down and become withdrawn.

- **Criticism can elicit defensiveness** – When confronted with criticism we can feel psychologically (and even physically) threatened. As a result, we attempt to deflect, defend, and justify — oftentimes even before fully assessing the content of the criticism. If we feel attacked we will work to defend our sense of self. The actual topic or substance of the criticism becomes secondary as we defend ourselves to regain or restore our balance.

All of this seems to suggest that criticism can be uncomfortable regardless of which side you are on; although we do tend to focus on the way criticism impacts us personally. Of course, this begs the question: Is it better to give or receive?

> *"One test of good manners is the ability to put up pleasantly with bad ones."*
> ~ W. Willkie

Is it Better to Give or Receive?

Interestingly, when addressing criticism, I believe the answer is both—with a few caveats. As we strive to retool the concept of criticism to be consistent with our new definition, the prospect of both giving and receiving criticism becomes a bit less perilous. There are a number of questions we can ask ourselves to determine if we are on the right path. When giving criticism are we focused on what we could do to help the other person become better? Will others know from our actions and demeanor that when we offer criticism it is intended to assist them to become more competent and productive? Are we focused on helping rather than blaming, censuring, or attacking their self-esteem? It is in this phase of deliberative preparation that the giver of criticism seems to have the most control. The critic should carefully consider how they are going to prepare and deliver the criticism in order to have the desired positive result; this is when they have the greatest influence. Once delivered, the options in managing criticism shift to the recipient.

The Potential in Receiving Criticism

When receiving criticism, do we direct our attention to assessing the information in such a way that allows us to extract the useful elements of another's comments? Are we able to appraise the criticism on its merits rather than its emotion? Can we accept that criticism can be both hurtful and helpful? Many people erroneously believe that all the "strength" in the criticism cycle lies in giving criticism. Something akin to seeing the critic as a potentially benevolent dictator (or worse) whose words will fall like a thud on the hapless recipient. Those who offer criticism do have the positional power in the conversation—initially. The critic determines what they want to convey, how they want to say it, and when they will offer their criticism. The critic, by choice of word and deed, can deliver the criticism with either greater or lesser regard for the recipient; however, it is ultimately the recipient who has the ability to assess the criticism and the choice in the manner of response. Once the criticism has left the mouth of the critic, it cannot be recast or ushered back. As they say, you can't un-ring the bell or unscramble the eggs. The power of the criticism communication cycle now clearly shifts to the recipient. The recipient will be able to exercise their discretion in how to listen, evaluate, acknowledge, respond, and navigate their success in managing the criticism. (The L.E.A.R.N. Method that we will discuss in later chapters.) Both roles of giving and receiving are critical in effectively offering productive and constructive criticism; however, recipients often feel they have the heavier burden of managing the criticism. As we will see, they also have greater latitude in responding.

Self-Criticism: It's Giving *and* Receiving

Self-criticism can be particularly difficult as we are both the giver and receiver of critical information through our own self-evaluation and self-talk; we are saying these things about *ourselves*. Research has shown that we are often not objective in our examination of the issues and we often focus on the negative to the exclusion of all else. In fact, this overly and overtly negative orientation is a key feature of criticism of both self and others. Interestingly, there may be a biological-historical value in focusing on the negative or the threat. For example, when hiking through the woods, it is likely more valuable to focus on plants and animals that can *kill* you rather than on things that are more innocuous in order to maintain your longevity. Unfortunately this negative focus can take its toll on our interpersonal relationships. Have you ever noticed that housework, for example, is something that is seldom noticed unless left undone! We seldom think about the fact that the floors are vacuumed, the dishes are clean, and the clothes are washed. We only notice it when we see a spot on the carpet, we don't have a clean bowl for our cereal, or our favorite shirt is in the hamper rather than on the hanger.

Clearly we cannot eliminate our own internal dialogue, but we can work to address it more effectively. Some use self-critical thought to move them into action, some use it to procrastinate, others use it to motivate; if you use it to find those things on which you can improve that is great. As with most other aspects of dealing with self-criticism, the key is to evaluate and assess; appraise whether what you are saying to yourself is fair, accurate, and tells the complete story. It may be based on a relatively insignificant comment from the perspective of another that we unfairly overweigh or on an incomplete understanding of events. Ask yourself: How accurate is the information? From whom did you receive the information? Is it based on facts or conclusions? Is there a likelihood of other information of which I am unaware that might sway my perception? What other considerations are there for this event? Does this address a problem or a symptom? Can I do anything about it? Am I fairly assessing the whole situation?

With self-criticism the big problem is the potential for continuous "Woulda, Coulda, Shoulda" ruminations. Although it may be true that there were other things that could have been done differently, we all make mistakes and it is seldom productive to relive them over and over. The goal is to better assess what might be helpful in the *future* rather than continually beating yourself up over something that happened in the past which you cannot change.

As we move forward, our goal is to further reconsider our concept of criticism from the perspectives of both the giver and the recipient. Instead of trepidation and anxiety, perhaps we can engender a sense of cooperation and growth. We can better conceptualize the criticism construction process and consider specific techniques to both give and receive criticism more productively. However, before getting into the specifics of giving, receiving, and seeking criticism, we should first consider the myriad of issues that influence the criticism communication process. In a recent study, underlying communication problems were identified as the key contributor to ineffective criticism.[4] If we can develop more effective criticism communication skills, both giving and receiving criticism can be much more productive.

Chapter 4
Critical Communications: Problems and Processes

"I know you understand what you think I said, I'm just not sure if what you heard was exactly what I meant." ~ *Unknown*

A Word, Please
Criticism Particulars
Writing Makes it Right?
Biases, Filters, and Preconceptions...Oh My
It's Not What You Said
Did you Listen or Just Hear?
Effective Criticism Communication

Whether we are clear or not, we are *always* communicating. Even as you sit and read, you are in some way communicating your level of interest in this book, or your disinterest in other things around you. I tell members of my college classes and professional seminars that every moment they are sitting in class, they are communicating. Communication is by far more complicated than simple verbal interaction. It is a complex process of symbols, meanings, gestures, interactions, and interpretations that can be fraught with problems and errors. Criticism is clearly a communication event. As such we need to consider influences that can impact this process.

Communication can be formally defined as a giving or exchange of information, signals, symbols, or messages by talking, gesturing, or writing. For the communication to be effective, the recipient must have in his or her mind the message that was intended by the sender. Of course this is not always an easy proposition. The message can be distorted by any number of factors including "noise" or the communication method that has been selected.

"The two words "information" and "communication" are often used interchangeably, but they signify quite different things. Information is giving out; communication is getting through."
~ Sydney J. Harris

In the communication model we can see that we begin with a message that must be communicated by some means such as gesture, writing, words, or symbols; this is the communication channel. This is our first opportunity for problems as the channel itself may be faulty. For example, the sender may choose written correspondence as the communication channel; however the sender may have extraordinarily poor handwriting. The poor handwriting creates communication "noise" that impedes an effective interaction. Further, the recipient may have poor eyesight or have forgotten their reading glasses and may not be able to decipher the message; so the receiver channel is also hampering the communication process. The end result: there is no effective communication. Of course, the best way to determine if the message sent is the message received is by soliciting feedback. However, as we will see in later chapters, the *way* that feedback is addressed in criticism communications can be critical to success.

Suppose that you were trying to communicate to someone on the opposite side of a very noisy, busy street. You may use a variety of means including yelling and gestures; however, in this case, the actual noise of the communication environment may prevent the recipient from getting the message. Additionally, the poor hearing of the recipient or the sore throat and weak voice of the sender can impact the receiver and communication channels, respectively.

Communication Process

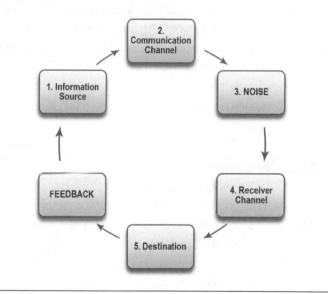

In another example, let's say you are in rush hour traffic and some inconsiderate jerk cuts you off. Perhaps your first choice of communication might be verbal; however, it is doubtful that effective communication could occur as the intended recipient will likely not be able to hear you. Moreover, he may not be attending to you at all. Alternatively, you may choose to offer a hand gesture to the other driver indicating your displeasure with his apparent callous behavior. What possible barriers to communication might occur here? Well, the symbol may be unknown to the recipient (doubtful); the intended recipient may not be looking your way at the time of the offering; or possibly the recipient may be looking your way, but—fortunately for you as you now see this guy is the size of a Philistine weightlifter—the tinted windows in your vehicle prevents the reception of your intended "message." (Sometimes communication errors may not be all bad!) In each case the noise involved in the communication process impeded the intended result.

Of course communication noise can come in many forms. As it relates to dealing with criticism, the emotional state of the giver or the recipient can create psychological noise. The sender may choose a tone, method, or word choice that may not be well received by the individual to whom the criticism is directed. The recipient may "hear" a more negative message than was intended as a result of emotional arousal.

A Word, Please

In particular, word choice can be vital to effective communication when dealing with criticism. In the English language the 500 most commonly used words have over 14,000 definitions! (Interestingly, English has the most words of any language, approximately 616,500; although the average person only uses about 60,000 throughout their lifetime.) Additionally, a particular word may change with the context of the speaker, the listener, or the circumstance. For example, the word "joint" can have many meanings depending on the situation. If a police officer (speaker) is talking to a junkie (listener) in the jail cell (circumstance), chances are the discussion is about an illegal substance. However, if a plumber (speaker) is talking to a customer (listener) in his rapidly flooding basement (circumstance), we are probably talking about a pipe (not to be confused with a pipe that could be used in the previous example). Similarly, an orthopedist is likely referring to a body part, a correctional warden is likely talking about prison, an alcoholic may be referring to a beer joint, and a lawyer may be referring to a child custody arrangement. It is no wonder English as a Second Language (ESL) classes can be so difficult.

Words themselves typically have a *denotation*, the literal meaning of the term, and a *connotation*, a nuance, subtext, or feeling. As a result, word choice can be critical when attempting to convey a certain tone or ambiance. For example, "home" tends to have a somewhat positive connotation for most, relating to thoughts of family and friends. In contrast, the synonym "house" tends to elicit thoughts of a structure or edifice. Depending on the intended message, the choice between these two words can be important. Mark Twain said "the difference between the right word and the *almost* right word is the difference between 'lightning' and 'lightning bug.'" Especially when communicating criticism, word selection can be crucial. You would not want to create an unintended consequence by using an overly emotion-laden word when a less reactive word would work best.

To further muddy the waters, consider words such as "inexcusable," meaning *not* excusable, or "inappropriate," meaning *not* appropriate. Now contrast that with words such as "inflammable" or "invaluable"; despite the similar prefix these words mean *very* flammable and *very* valuable, respectively. As critical as word choice is to the already difficult process of communicating criticism, it is essential to recognize the potential complexity. *How* someone communicates a message through manner and means (such as word choice) can be even more important than the content of the message itself.

> *"The most important thing in communication is to hear what isn't being said."* ~ *Peter Drucker*

Word choice in phrases or statements can have a dramatic impact on the effectiveness of the communication. Below are several phrases that are often used in providing criticism and alternatives that may be better accepted by the recipient. Oftentimes this involves offering less assertive or less absolute language. This can be particularly problematic (depending on context) with words such as "always," "never," "anything," "everything," "nothing," and so forth. Typically, people do not *always* mess up, they don't fail at *everything*, and they usually are not in a position to *never* do *anything* right or to be "good for *nothing*." Using words in such a manner is pejorative, inaccurate, and likely to elicit defensiveness.

When considering criticism we should recognize that we may not always be aware of the entire story or the complete circumstance. As a result, offering less conclusive words, phrases, or statements—at least initially—can help to reduce potential defensiveness. By taking a less definitive position, particularly in the initial phases of the conversation, you are psychologically signaling that there is a room for a dialogue or discussion, rather than a one-way monologue in which you have already made up your mind regarding the situation and the outcome.

Alternative Phrasing for Success

Phrase
"You said…."
Better Phrase
"I thought we agreed…"

Phrase
"It is absolutely certain…"
Better Phrase
"It appears to me that…"

Phrase
"I know for a fact that…"
Better Phrase
"It seems that…"

Phrase
"You are wrong…"
Better Phrase:
"I have a different perspective…"

Phrase
"You never…"
Better Phrase
"It would be great if…"

Phrase
"You have definitely…"
Better Phrase
"As I understand it…"

Phrase
"You always…"
Better Phrase
"I've noticed…"

Phrase
"If you had not done that…"
Better Phrase
"In the future…"

Phrase
"Why did you do it like that?"
Better Phrase
"What do you think about doing it like this?"

Notice that in most cases, the first, more absolute and potentially pejorative phrasing is past-oriented and assumes you are the sole arbitrator of facts and information. The alternative phrasing is often more future-oriented and leaves open the possibility of alternative explanations or information. We don't always have the complete picture and we can do little about what has already happened; however, we can look to the future to address what went wrong or ways to perform better.

Criticism Particulars

When it comes to emotion-laden criticism there are a few other word-choice caveats for us to consider. For example, "You" statements, particularly those that are accusatory, can be a problem because they tend to focus the criticism on the individual. "*You* really made a mess of things!" "*You* did this all wrong!" "*You* are a …!" This places the criticism spotlight back on the person, not the actual behavior. A rule I learned a long time ago was to primarily use "you" statements for positives such as, "You really did a great job!" or "You are doing very well!" (You = Positive). If you are addressing a concern or criticism, it is often better to phrase it from your perspective with "I" statements, such as "I am concerned that…" or "I am worried that…." Then follow that with the fact-based specifics that focus on the behavior. (I = Concern). Of course, it is not really possible to eliminate the pronoun "you" from your vocabulary—that makes no practical sense. What we are talking about here is the use of the term in an accusatory or intentionally harsh manner that is often focused on casting blame.

"Ninety percent of the friction of daily life is caused by the wrong tone of voice."
~ Francois de la Rochefoucauld

Additionally, terms like "but" and "however," (depending on usage and context) can tend to elicit disagreement and dichotomous thinking. Both figuratively and grammatically "but" statements can negate everything that came before them. In fact, in computer programming "but" statements are designed to negate previous information and commands. The use of the conjunction "and" is by far a more suitable choice. For example, you might start a conversation off with something like, "I want you to know that I really appreciate all of your efforts aimed at improvement *and* I think you can be even more effective if…" Now consider this example phrase again, only this time use the word "but" in the place of "and." Which do you feel sounds more helpful or encouraging?

Writing Makes it Right?

Some people suggest that the most effective way to ensure that there is no confusion in the communication process is to write everything down. The belief is that there is less room for error if the information is presented in this tangible form. Of course, we have already seen that writing as a communication channel can be problematic; for example if the sender has illegible handwriting. Additionally, as a practical matter, it is unlikely that most of us could go through the day communicating only by writing, and in the context of criticism communications it could actually be disastrous.

In fact, writing may not clarify the intent of the message, as the recipient must filter it through their own perceptual filters and biases. When someone reads a written message, depending on which word or words they emphasize when interpreting the information, the result may be much different than was intended. For example, look at the following message:

"I did not say you took too many breaks when you worked last Friday night."

In this message the meaning can shift when the emphasis is placed on different words. Perhaps the person wishes to deny any involvement in such a statement if confronted. In this case, if the focus is on the word "say" the person may be thinking, "I didn't *say* it; I wrote a memo." If the focus is on "you" they may be thinking "I didn't say *you*; I said everyone on that shift." If the attention of the message is directed to the words "last Friday," for example, the person may rationalize that they didn't say *last* Friday; just some recent Friday. Again, simply writing a message does not ensure communication clarity, as the wording must be interpreted by the recipient.

Biases, Filters, and Preconceptions...Oh My

One of the most important considerations in dealing with others is the recognition that people typically see things not as they actually are, but as the person *is*. This is one of the fundamental lessons of social psychology. In other words, people process everything through their own emotional and perceptual filters. As a result, a criticism of one's paper in a college class, for example, that merely suggests it "needs a little work" can be processed by an individual in an overly emotional or sensitive state as "it's a complete, worthless mess."

There are dozens of cognitive and perceptual biases and errors to which we all fall prey on occasion. The study of social psychology in particular demonstrates how a group of people can see the same phrase, thing, or event, and yet individuals within the group come away with completely different impressions or opinions. The point is that others will not necessarily (and likely will not) see the world in the same way that you might. One interesting study that illuminated this situation involved individuals who were asked to wear a sandwich board sign around a college campus for 15 minutes.[5] A sandwich board sign is one of those large advertising signs that has a panel on the front and back and is fitted over the wearer, usually by shoulder straps. (Think of the old sidewalk pitchmen that wore the "Eat at Joes'" type sign.) Interestingly, those who agreed to wear the sign believed that most other people would also wear the sign if asked. Conversely, those that refused to wear the sign believed that most others would also refuse. It seems that we tend to suffer from what has been termed the False Consensus Effect—the belief that our opinion is shared by most others.

The psychological area of attribution theory is also particularly salient to the topic of criticism. Attribution theory examines how people explain other's behavior, usually by attributing it (thus, the name) to some internal disposition—such as their personality or character—or to external, situational forces. However, what researchers most find is that we have a strong tendency to attribute the cause of another's behavior to personal traits or characteristics and often neglect, minimize, or ignore situational explanations. This has been termed the

Fundamental (because we all do it) Attribution Error.[6] For example, when we *receive* unexpected criticism, we can quickly create a story—almost always negative— that explains the actions of the critic as being a product of their self-centered, hostile, uninformed, mean-spirited nature. When we are in a position to *offer* criticism, we often attribute the problem in their performance to their inconsiderate, lazy, inattentive, or careless disposition rather than some less insidious situational factor.

The Fundamental Attribution Error has its roots in another related cognitive heuristic known as the Actor-Observer Bias. This bias suggests that when *we* act, we tend to focus on the *situation* (I tripped because there is a crack in the sidewalk). When we *observe* others act, we often ignore the contributing factors of the situation and focus solely on the character of that *individual*—usually in a negative way (You tripped because you are a klutz). As a result, when someone is criticized, their first reaction may be to ignore the possible situational factors (including that the criticism is accurate) and focus instead on the critic's perceived lack of civility and other presumed character flaws. If we are the one offering the criticism, our first response may be to only focus on the perceived flaws within the person and ignore other situation factors that might explain the behavior or circumstance. For example, if we notice that a coworker comes in late, we might automatically assume that they are lazy, apathetic, and inconsiderate of others—all things related to their *character*. However, what we may not realize is that this person has a sick child that requires extra attention each morning—a *situational* explanation. Further, in our cognitive rush to judgment, we may also be unaware that the coworker has told the supervisor of the problem and has received permission to arrive a little late. We have a cognitive bias to focus on the char-

Critical Communications: Problems and Processes

acter of the person, not the circumstance. As a result, we create our judgment absent full information or facts.

Although an in-depth examination of these cognitive biases and errors is beyond the scope of this book, a review of a good social psychology textbook could prove to be invaluable (that is, *very* valuable).

It's Not What You Said

It's frequently the case that messages, especially those that are potentially emotion-laden, are interpreted by the recipient based more on *how* the information is communicated. *Nonverbal communication* can play a major role in the criticism communication process. Facial expressions, body language, eye contact, vocal tone, and interpersonal distance can all contribute to the interpretation of a message. The six basic *facial expressions* (anger, happiness, sadness, disgust, fear, and surprise) are actually biologically determined. That is, regardless of societal influences these facial expressions are interpretable across cultures. In fact, even infants can distinguish among these expressions. What are less predetermined are the display rules that tend to be culturally influenced. For example, in America women tend to smile more than men and men tend to cry less than women, at least in public. These are the "rules" with which we grew up. Of course there is great variation among individuals and these displays are subject to inaccurate interpretation. For example, smiling may be a sign of happiness or may equally be a sign of nervousness. Crying may be from pain or as a result of joy. Again, the communication process is complex.

Body language is often more pop psychology than science. However, this pop psychology has become a part of our culture and people believe it to be true. For example, despite a great deal of empirical evidence that sitting with your arms lightly crossed is really unrelated to your attention to a speaker, many believe that it is a signal that you have disconnected with the speaker and the message, that you are creating a physical and emotional barrier. As a result, when we find ourselves in criticism-prone situations, we must be mindful of the perception rather than the reality of such a posture.

Eye contact is another often misunderstood component of nonverbal communication. Although it does seem to be true that eye contact can be useful in regulating turn-taking in a conversation (think about it, if you do not want to be interrupted as you see the other person is about to speak, most people will look away to maintain their speaking position), there is little credence that someone who is not constantly "looking you in the eye" is being untruthful. In fact, it may be a sign of deference to status or an indication of nervousness. It is true, however, that women tend to engage in more eye contact than men and males tend to engage in more visual dominance posturing, looking or keeping eye contact more with a person considered to be lower status than one who might be considered higher status. Again, if you are communicating critical information it is likely a good idea to look at your subject lest they think you are being less than honest; after all, that is what we have been told for years.

"By inflection you can say much more than your words do." ~ *Malcolm Forbes*

Vocal tone can have a dramatic impact on the recipient's interpretation of verbal information. The harshness or softness of tone, the emphasis of certain words, as well as the speed of delivery can all influence the content of the message. While the emphasis and volume of tone are obvious in their effect, the idea of speed is less intuitive. Interestingly, studies have demonstrated that

Critical Communications: Problems and Processes

people who speak faster versus slower are perceived as more credible. Of course, this does not account for the near imperceptibly fast talkers like those in the FedEx commercials many years ago. Instead, those who speak in a clear, quick pace are seen as more trustworthy. This may be a result of being confident—so there is no halting speech pattern—or may be due to the pace of the message exceeding the recipients' capacity to consider counter arguments, as has been suggested in some studies.

Interpersonal distance clearly has a cultural component, as well as an occupational one. People in France, for example, tend to stand much closer during conversations than those in the US or the UK. Germans tend to stand much further apart when talking than most other nationalities. Occupationally, police officers, for example, tend to have a larger interpersonal distance than most others. This is likely due to training and survival skill preparation. Clearly, when trying to effectively communicate with another, it is best to respect such social norms.

Of course, when we communicate with others we typically use many different communication channels. Some research has suggested that emotional messages are primarily communicated through nonverbal channels. Interestingly, when nonverbal cues and the actual message are in conflict, most people focus on the nonverbal when interpreting the message. A person who says "That was great!" but does so with crossed arms, clinched fists, harsh tone, and a stern scowl is likely to be most accurately interpreted from the nonverbal communication cues.

Did You Listen or Just Hear?

One of the most critical aspects of any communication process is found in the art of active or empathetic listening. That is, listening for meaning, understanding, and with the intent to truly comprehend the speaker. All too often we are so concerned with formulating our own reply, especially if we are put on the defensive, that we do not truly hear the message. Only if you fully concentrate on attending to the speaker and thoughtfully listen to their message will you be able to properly respond.

"The greatest gift you can give another is the purity of your attention."
~ Richard Moss, MD

Active listening is a skill that is seldom taught, seldom emphasized, and seldom practiced. We were all involved in some sort of speech class during our education or were involved in providing a "show and tell" or asked to speak to the class on what we did during summer vacation. We are provided with many opportunities in our formal education to learn to speak and write more effectively; however, we are less likely to have been exposed to a class that focused on listening skills. Listening is not the same as hearing. Hearing is a physiological process of converting sound waves into recognizable units for our brains to interpret. Listening is centered on adding meaning, content, and context to those words; it is what provides the significance to the communication process. Active listening takes effort; after all, we have to work to undo years of training. However, those who listen well are perceived to be more knowledgeable, more fair, and are viewed as more valuable friends. Think about people in your own life whom you consider to be good listeners and emulate them. A person who commits to truly listening with empathy and understanding makes a valuable contribution in the lives of others. This becomes all the more important when we are dealing with potentially emotional issues in criticism-prone situations. As givers of criticism we cannot be sure of the accuracy of our position unless we have been open to listening; as recipients of criticism we cannot expect to respond effectively until we fully understand the position of our critic and the motivation they have for offering their comments. If you do not engage in active listening, how will you assess what the critic has offered and how will you know if your own criticism is valid?

I am sure we've all heard the term active listening, but we seldom receive actual advice on what it really involves. Obviously it includes carefully listening to the words, comments, meaning, and cues of others. However, we likely need to place a greater emphasis on the *active* part. From my perspective one of the very best ways to listen for understanding is to ask questions. As I discuss elsewhere, using appropriate questions can be one of the best ways to understand, to communicate, and to even offer criticism. When you are listening to another you are likely formulating questions in your own mind. For example, you may ask yourself: How did they come to that conclusion? What information do they have that I do not? Why do they feel so strongly? How or why do they see things differently than I do?

One great thing about asking questions in the active listening process is that it allows you to begin assessing information. If you are *receiving* criticism, asking questions can allow you to better understand the critic, their criticism, and the perspectives. Interestingly, when we begin to think in terms of asking questions when confronted with criticism, we also tend to be a bit less defensive. Because we are concentrating on gaining a better understanding, we are less prone to solely focus on our emotional response. We are short-circuiting some of the rather automatic cognitive responses and are spending more effort with cognitive functioning (brain power). If you are preparing to *offer* criticism, asking questions of yourself and others can allow you to consider added information, biases, or perceptions that may be influencing you. Better to ask a few questions that stimulate your thinking and address possible misunderstandings *before* launching off with potentially uninformed comments. In fact, as we will discuss more fully later, when one does offer criticism it is often a good idea to end the initial conversation with a question. For example, after factually explaining your observations (not absolute conclusions) you might say something like: "It seems to me that this violated our company policy. Do I have that correct or is there something I'm missing?" or "...given the state of this report, it appears that the quality is not what we expect. Is there something going on here that I am not aware of?" Similar to our discussion on using less assertive language and taking a less definitive position, particularly in the initial phases of a criticism conversation, asking such questions psychologically signals that there is a room for other reasonable opinions or explanations. It lets the other person know that you are fairly considering the entire situation and are open to additional or alternative information—that could provide you with insight that can alter your views. We will discuss this further in later chapters.

Effective Criticism Communication

Effective communication skills are essential in the criticism management process. In fact, numerous management studies reveal that strong communication abilities are synonymous with leadership success. When encountering the sensitive area of criticism-prone communications, the process can be all the more challenging. Several specific suggestions are offered throughout this book that are designed to elicit a more productive communication process.

When considering criticism, we also need to be aware of how some of the psychological biases and cognitive errors that we have already considered can interact with the entire communication process, both our internal processing and external interactions. In the next chapter we will explore the Criticism Corridor, the psychological paths that can impact our thinking, understanding, and response when dealing with criticism.

Chapter 5
The Criticism Corridor: The Path to Problems

"It is unfair to criticize that which you don't understand." ~ *Abraham Lincoln*

The Criticism Corridor
The Paul Harvey Solution
Critical Contributions

The Criticism Corridor

Criticism often follows a somewhat predicable, reactive path and many of the psychological biases and processing errors discussed in the previous chapters tend to kick-in. Such biases can cause us to misinterpret, misunderstand, misread, and misconstrue the events or circumstance. For example, when we are criticized we often—and without much effort or mindful processing—create an unflattering story about the critic and the criticism. We focus on the negative as a defensive reaction to a perceived threat and our characterization of the critic is often the result of the Fundamental Attribution Error addressed in Chapter 4. Our first reaction is to ignore the possible situational factors (including that the criticism is accurate or the critic is properly addressing the concern) and instead focus on perceived character flaws of the critic. After all, only an inconsiderate, self-absorbed jerk would dare to criticize me! Unfortunately, this near automatic story tends to elicit a near automatic emotional response, which in-turn often results in a behavioral reaction (word or deed). As a result, we find ourselves traveling through the Criticism Corridor as illustrated below.[1]

Receive Criticism — Create Attributional Story — Story Elicits Emotion — We Act / React

Of course the problem is that there are many potential flaws with our story and with all that follows. We each have different filters, histories, and experiences that guide and color our interpretations. So what we notice or what directs our attention can be as varied as the person involved. Additionally, we often infer the intentions of others based on the impact of their actions. In other words, if someone criticizes us in a way that we perceive to be adversely impactful to our self-esteem, for example, we will infer that they did this intentionally. It doesn't really matter if the critic tried to be tactful; what matters is how *we* assess or appraise their motives and the situation. Never mind that we can't, at that instant, really know their intentions—we don't have access to their private thoughts. Yet, we have no problem attributing a host of ills to their character. To further add to the mix, we are typically great at jumping to conclusions. (In fact, for some of us, jumping to conclusions is the only exercise we get!) Again, all of this can happen in a split second. Notice that this process is occurring between our ears and behind our eyes—it is all in our head at this point.

> *"If choice must be made between rationality and fervor; men will choose fervor."*
> ~ *George A. Buttrick*

So we receive criticism and then the cognitive defensive wheels begin to churn. We create defensive stories often based on incomplete information, faulty assumptions, and inferred intentions. These uncomplimentary, negatively-based stories elicit an emotional response which is often similarly unflattering. We get angry, irritated, annoyed, indignant, resentful, or any of a host of other emotional labels that we use. As a result of that emotion we are then likely to engage in some verbal or other behavior (counterattack, retaliation, backbiting, etc.)—all based on our potentially biased perceptions, flawed thinking, and faulty story.

In a similar way, when we are primed to *offer* criticism to others, we may follow a comparable pattern. We notice a behavior that we do not like or, if in a work environment, may violate a policy or standard. The observation, influenced by cognitive biases such as the Actor-Observer Bias and the Fundamental Attribution Error, (see Chapter 4) leads us to create a story as to the cause of their offending behavior. Again, this is a rather automatic process, not a reflective contemplation. The story we tell ourselves can lead to an emotional consequence. We may perceive, based on our potentially compromised and incomplete story that the individual acted with deliberate intention, thus eliciting an emotional response, not unlike the fight-or-flight syndrome. As a result of our likely imperfect observation, our incomplete attributional story, and our heightened emotional state, we may find ourselves poised for attack.

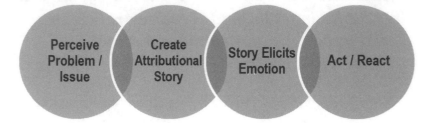

For example, consider a supervisor who noticed that an employee arrived for work late. The supervisor may immediately assume that the individual is lazy, inattentive, must not appreciate their job, and may even view this as a personal affront to their own supervisory authority. As a result, this story (as incomplete as it may be, as all they really know is that they believe the person was late) can elicit an emotional reaction. The supervisor may become indignant that a worker would slough-off their responsibilities on their watch. The supervisor may even begin to ruminate on how this unacceptable behavior jeopardizes his job and adversely impacts the other workers. Again, this process can occur in seconds; it is likely that it took much more time to read this sentence than it took for this process to unfold. Consequently, the supervisor may launch into a tirade of criticism aimed at the employee. Of course, the employee being on the receiving end, will often immediately experience the process mentioned above, quickly concluding that the supervisor is a rude, thoughtless, mean-spirited, critical jerk. This may be especially true if the tardy arrival was due to a family emergency, an unavoidable traffic delay, or any of a host of other circumstances that the supervisor did not bother to consider when creating their story.

"What really matters is what happens in us, not to us." ~ *James W. Kennedy*

Fortunately, this criticism-reaction sequence can be positively influenced. Studies have shown that people can become more aware of these biasing influences and work to mitigate their impact. We can learn to slow down our aversive reactions in criticism-prone situations by considering other potential influences and we can work to cognitively reframe the entire process. Keep in mind that *we* are the ones who are creating the story that leads to the counterproductive response. As a result, we can take control by considering a different story or by offering a different version of the events. We can strive to become more aware of the attributional biases and their impact. We can infer different intentions. We can assign different meanings. We can ask questions of ourselves and others *before* we create a caustic conclusion. We can rethink our own story.

The Paul Harvey Solution

The late Paul Harvey (his full name was Paul Harvey Aurandt) was a famous radio broadcaster and personality. He was best known for his home-spun style, his folksy delivery, and his signature vocal inflections and dramatic pauses. He would often have an unusual or humorous story as a part of his broadcast that had a curious or quirky conclusion. After setting up the story, he would then say "and now...the *rest* of the story" thereafter revealing the frequently peculiar ending. (In fact, he wrote a book titled *The Rest of the Story*.)

As it relates to the process of handling criticism, we can take a page from Paul Harvey and tell ourselves *the rest of the story*. Much of the problem with the criticism corridor described above comes as a result of our incomplete, biased, or inaccurate story. However, if we take steps to generate a more complete story — one that more accurately assesses what is fact versus what might be premature conclusion — we can create a more accurate version that may be less likely to elicit the adverse emotional and behavioral consequences.

First we need to *slow down*; there is usually no need to rush to judgment. In such matters as this, people rarely regret their silences—more likely they regret their premature reactions based on faulty or incomplete information. Second, we need to put our thinking in reverse *before* saying or doing anything. Ask yourself: Why am I irritated or upset? What emotion am I feeling? Why do I have that emotion? What is it based on? Third, consider the story that you have created. Was your rendition based on facts or supposition? How has your version of the story lead to the emotions? How did you develop your story? Finally, consider your own observations, biases, inferences, contributions, and other elements that went into your account. What did you actually see or hear? What inferences did you make? What information could you be missing? What situational factors could be involved? What might the other person know about the situation that you do not?

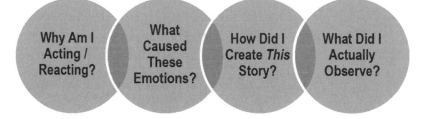

An individual once told me about a situation in which he had been trying to get in touch with a coworker on an important project. Despite leaving numerous e-mails and phone messages, he did not receive even the courtesy of a reply. He became incensed at this insensitive and inconsiderate behavior. He began imagining all sorts of negative things about this individual—including that the person was intentionally sabotaging the project

The Criticism Corridor: The Path to Problems

and trying to make him look bad. His phone calls and e-mails went ballistic. Accusations, criticism, name calling, and colorful language were peppered throughout. His perception of the situation led to his creation of an attributional story which, in turn, elicited strong emotions and his caustic behavior. He was clearly down the rocky path of the Criticism Corridor. Now, here is the rest of the story. The co-worker was not out to get his job, was not trying to make anyone look bad, and was not intentionally sabotaging anything. The co-worker was actually in a state of shock, as he was attending to his wife's funeral after she had unexpectedly died a few days before, leaving a husband and three young children behind. After learning the real situation, imagine what was now going through the mind of our "critic." He was embarrassed and mortified by his behavior. He was accusing another of being inconsiderate, yet he was the one who jumped to conclusions, inferred intention based on impact, and created an entire negative scenario—without the benefit of accurate information and facts. He told me he was so ashamed he quit his job and has never been the same since. However, he relates that he now is acutely aware of his negative-thinking tendencies and says he has become a "master" at slowing down his thinking when he begins to wander through the elements of the Criticism Corridor. It would have been doubly tragic if he experienced this life-changing event and did not benefit from the life-lesson. Experience can be a valuable, but expensive teacher.

When we consider the Paul Harvey Solution we are committing to work toward a more complete understanding of others and their actions. We are working to diminish the impact of cognitive biases and influences. We are establishing guides to help better assess and appraise the situation. We are becoming better at constructing the criticism we give and assessing the criticism we receive because we are focused on acknowledging that there is more than we might have first considered—we are now considering "the rest of the story."

Critical Contributions

One of the ways we can better focus on creating a more accurate interpretation of critical events is to consider our own contributions. This often starts by first moving past the "blame game" and considering issues that are likely more meaningful. Blame is more about judging rather than understanding. Blame focuses on the past; contributions tend to focus on future-based solutions. Blame is like a lamppost for drunks, it provides support rather than illumination. Blame is often used to support the punitive position of the critic; it does not explain, enlighten, or clarify.

"Figure out **what** *went wrong, not* **who** *was wrong, when communication breaks down."*
~ Tom Nash

When considering our contributions to criticism-prone situations, we ask ourselves: What might I have done to contribute to this situation? What would the other person say was my contribution to the current circumstance? How have my actions factored into this event? Is there some practice or policy impacting this situation? Considering contributions is not about assessing right and wrong; it is about capturing the elements that led to the current situation.

For example, assume that you are the supervisor in the earlier scenario who observes that an employee is coming in late for work. In order to assess any potential contribution, you must consider what role, if any, you or your policies may have played. Perhaps others have occasionally come in late to work without penalty. Perhaps this person has intermittently come in late to work in the past, but has never been questioned. These are potential contributions. As a result of failing to take any corrective action in the past, you have, in effect, created a practice or informal policy that suggests occasional tardiness is not a concern. To offer criticism for these actions now without acknowledging this contribution would be disingenuous at best. A better course of action would be to first acknowledge that past attendance practices have been a bit lax and explain that you need to make a change. By first accepting responsibility for a part of the problem, you set the tone for the future without unfairly holding others solely accountable for a circumstance that clearly involved contributions from both sides.

When we acknowledge our own accountability, minimize blame, and consider our own contributions our path to more effectively handing criticism becomes much less rocky. In the next chapter, we will begin to incorporate the issues we have covered in the previous chapters and consider more specific steps involved in providing productive and constructive criticism to others.

The Criticism Corridor: The Path to Problems

Chapter 6
Constructing Criticism: Putting the P.C. into Criticism (No, Not Political Correctness)

"Criticism should not be querulous and wasting, all knife and root-puller, but guiding, instructive, inspiring." ~ Ralph Waldo Emerson

The Art of Giving Criticism: Being P.C.
Before Giving Criticism
Have the Proper Mindset
   (*If you don't read anything else about giving criticism to others...read this!*)

How do you provide criticism to others? How do you react if someone does or says something that you really don't like? Do you zap them with stinging comments? If you do, how might this affect the long-term relationship with that person? While it is true that we can sometimes gain a measure of satisfaction by letting someone have it with both barrels, such guilty pleasure is often short-lived. Giving someone a strong rebuke, especially if we feel they truly deserve it, can be satisfying—the problem is that it's not particularly successful in the long run. We must focus on the ultimate goal in providing criticism to others. Ask yourself, is your objective to allow *you* to *temporarily* feel better by venting, or is it to be effective in helping another to grow, recover, improve, prosper, or excel (G.R.I.P.E.)? Especially in cases where another's behavior seems particularly egregious or you feel personally attacked, it is only natural to feel the desire for some form of verbal retribution; however, the greater goal and more important guiding principle must be to consider what the best course of action is when you contemplate the big picture. Sometimes things said in the heat of the moment are not particularly productive or reflective. Again, it is usually not our contemplative silences that we regret.

"It takes two years to learn to talk and seventy years to learn to control your mouth." ~ *Mark Twain*

The Art of Giving Criticism: Being P.C.

As we discussed earlier, our new characterization of criticism involves helping others to grow, recover, improve, prosper, or excel. If we recognize that the outcome of our criticism should be to help others succeed, we can appreciate the importance of making sure our criticism is P.C. No, not politically correct (as is seemingly overstated in today's environment), but focused on being *productive* and *constructive*. In fact, recall that our new definition of criticism is *offering productive and constructive information intended to help others grow, recover, improve, prosper, or excel.*

Providing effective criticism to others can be challenging and is usually *not* the most efficient communication technique. However, efficiency takes a backseat to long term effectiveness in the areas of critical communications. We all want critics to be thoughtful in their criticism of our actions, considering how *best* to communicate their message rather than how *quickly* it can be done. As mentioned previously, you can be efficient with things, but you must strive for effectiveness when dealing with people.

Although many focus on the difficulty of receiving criticism, giving criticism can be equally troubling. In fact, a recent survey of supervisors and executives indicated that giving criticism to subordinates was even more stressful than receiving criticism and complaints from others.[2] Giving criticism causes us to recognize that we may have to challenge others by telling them information that they may not wish to hear. We all have a desire to be liked, and we recognize that giving criticism can often be in conflict with that desire. People whose roles require that they provide criticism to others also indicate that they often have a sense of dread about the process—anticipating the confrontational nature of the encounter. In one study,[3] participants expressed concern that they might lose emotional control, they may feel out-of-balance with their upbringing that focused on sparing the feelings of others and being a "nice guy," and they frequently cite their lack of training and skill in effectively delivering criticism—something this book is clearly intended to address.

Many of these concerns can be diminished, if not alleviated, by reflectively and carefully considering the goal of criticism, the significance of our redefinition of criticism, and maintaining respect for the recipient. To effectively provide productive and constructive criticism, one should consider a number of important steps—even before uttering a single word. Preparation and consideration (yet another P.C.) are the keys. Effective criticism is not necessarily a matter of being a smooth talking diplomat; rather it is focused on sincerity, empathy, and integrity. Remember the goal is to help the person to whom you are offering the criticism (G.R.I.P.E.) which is not something easily done when "shooting from the hip." Just as there is a beginning, a middle, and an end to a book or story, to be more effective in walking through the potential minefield of providing criticism to others, one needs to consider three important phases: what to do *before*, *during*, and *after* providing criticism. The remainder of this chapter will focus on some of the things we should consider before offering criticism to others.

"What happens to the bee if it uses its sting is well known." ~ Dag Hammarskjold

---

Before Giving Criticism

Even before you utter a word, you must reflect on your motivation, your goal, the best approach, and the process of offering productive and constructive criticism. The following considerations can help you to formulate your productive and constructive criticism plan. These suggestions were gleaned from a large group of participants from a variety of vocational backgrounds, including clergy, business, public service, education, health care, and policing professionals.[3] Thus, these ideas were forged from the fires of experience in real world settings.

1. Consider Your Goal and Motivation

What is it that you want to accomplish with your criticism? Is your goal to help someone grow, recover, improve, prosper, or excel—as in our new definition of criticism? If you are not clear as to how your criticism will help the recipient, perhaps you should delay saying anything until you have unmistakably identified the benefit for the recipient. Additionally, you must be cognizant of your motivation for providing criticism. Even if the criticism could be helpful, it should likely not be offered when the motivation is less than honorable. If the underlying motivation is to put another in their place, or engage in an ego assault, it is best to allow those unproductive feelings to subside before offering your comments. In one study, people reported that "punishment" was one of the key motivations to offer criticism to another.[4] However, as we have already discussed, punishment falls far short of the ideal criticism communication.

"A good critic always brings something to his or her audience." ~ T.S. Eliot

---

2. Distill and Identify the Real Problem

To distill something means to refine, cull, extract, or condense it. Unfortunately, we don't always do a good job of making sure we are addressing the most concerning problem; often we are only attending to a symptom. This can be difficult because problems are often bound together and it can be tricky to tease apart the various components. You may have to peel away various layers of the proverbial onion in order to address the issue that is most concerning. One should be able to distill the actual problem into a single sentence, once you have fully analyzed the situation. Additionally, we need to recognize that the actual problem may change over time. For example, assume you have set a curfew for your son or daughter on evenings that they are allowed to go out with friends. If your son or daughter comes in late, you are *initially* dealing with a rule or curfew violation and you should address that specifically. If it occurs again, you are now set to address a *pattern or history* of behavior—something a bit different than the single occurrence. More importantly, however, if they come in late yet again and you are stuck on only addressing the rule violation—you have missed the boat. The real problem is *no longer about breaking the rules*; it is about the much more serious issues of trust, respect, and a loss of confidence—likely a much more concerning problem than the one with which you started.

3. Focus on Facts: Gather All the Relevant Information

Nothing could be worse than offering criticism that is unwarranted, undeserved, and based on faulty information. Before offering criticism you need to make sure you are dealing with *facts*, not your internal conclusions or attributional stories. Conclusions are about subjective judgments; conclusions are not facts. Your initial conclusions are more about what is going on between *your* ears and behind *your* eyes, not what the other person actually did or said. Much of Attribution Theory that we discussed in previous chapters has to do with these sorts of internal conclusions, judgments, and inferences. We nearly automatically attribute the behavior of another to their character or disposition and rarely consider other forces or factors that could account for their actions.

To more effectively offer productive and constructive criticism we need to make sure we have all of the relevant information that is based on *fact* not conjecture. Facts involve that which was actually observed—what you saw or what you heard. It focuses on the "what" not the "why." The "why" is more about your conclusions—often premature conclusions. When assessing facts it is also important to consider your own contributions or other possible factors involved in the issue. As indicated in the previous chapter, if practices or policies have contributed to the circumstance it would be hypocritical not to

Constructing Criticism

acknowledge it. Contributions could include organizational practices, past decisions, situational factors, peer pressure, different world views (such as generational difference) or any of a host of other circumstances. It is not that such influences necessarily excuses one's behavior; however, this information can provide additional insight and alternative explanations for the topic of the pending criticism—beyond our usual "default" position that it is all a result of their personality and character.

"Blame is safer than praise"
~ *Ralph Waldo Emerson*

Additionally, you must be cautious when you base criticism on information received from others. Many times those offering criticism (parents, supervisors, and so forth) may not have been present when the actual behavior occurred. As a result, we must be careful in our review of "facts" received by others. All of the biases and cognitive processing errors that affect you are also affecting them. They may report something in exaggerated detail, omit key elements, or explain things using provocative language. They may offer a pejorative perspective as a result of their own conclusions or emotional arousal. In order to gain the most relevant information from others, be sure you carefully ask for specifics—what was actually seen or heard, not relying on the second-hand conclusions of others. Ask others to speculate on other possible reasons for the individual's behavior as a way to widen their perspective. Whether relying on information from yourself or others, facts are essential in dealing with effective criticism. If you do not have the relevant, fact-based information, you are not prepared to offer criticism.

4. Consider the Time and Place

In order to effectively offer constructive and productive criticism, the time and location of the interaction must be considered. While some will suggest that feedback of all types, including criticism, is best if done immediately, I am not a particular fan of spur-of-the-moment criticism unless the giver is well experienced. Criticism that is immediate and not well thought out has the possibility of being overly emotional and harsh—not consistent with our goal of helping others improve (G.R.I.P.E.). The myth of immediacy has torpedoed many a well-intentioned critic.

The time of the day, location of the meeting, as well as the presence or absence of others are also important considerations. For example, a meeting at the end of a long and strenuous day might be ill advised. The timing must consider the emotional states of both the giver and receiver of criticism. Fatigue, irritability, or excessive emotionality can impede the effective delivery of criticism. Some management experts suggest that criticism is often best provided early in the day and early in the week. The idea is that this provides time for people to process the information and for other opportunities to interact in a less emotion-laden or casual context at other points in the day. It is less helpful to offer criticism at the proverbial "Friday at Five"—right before someone leaves for their weekend or days off. This can be emotionally straining and there is no opportunity to seek additional insight or information from the critic. It leaves the recipient "on their own" to ruminate about the criticism—as some of us know from experience, this can really kill your weekend!

The location involved in offering criticism may be dependent upon the relationship between the giver and receiver of the criticism. However, regardless of the relationship, typically an environment free from unnecessary distractions offers the greatest likelihood of creating a positive atmosphere. A busy hallway or a cluttered office subject to constant interruptions is usually no place to have a meeting in which critical information is exchanged.

"There is a time for everything and a season for every activity under Heaven"
~ Ecclesiastes (3:1)

In addition to these factors, the usual scenario in which criticism is given to another excludes the presence of others. The rule has traditionally been "praise in public, criticize in private." (Actually, we should advocate praising in public *and* in private!) Typically criticism is best handled in private. It is generally unprofessional and would run counter to the best interests of the recipient to criticize in a public venue. However, there are some unusual circumstances where the presence of others may be beneficial. For example, when a particular problem employee consistently misstates and misrepresents to others what you have said in private, you may be required to use another tactic. In this case the individual is intentionally escalating an adversarial environment, giving others a false perception of your style, demeanor, and integrity. In this case, well-crafted feedback in a public forum may be the best way to address the problem. Of course, this approach is not the first choice. Individuals typically have to "earn" the opportunity to receive correction in a more public setting as a consequence of their behavior.

5. Consider the Psychological and Emotional State of the Giver *and* the Recipient

If you or the recipient of the criticism are upset, fatigued, or emotionally exhausted there is a much greater chance that the criticism will come across as overly harsh or demeaning. Overly emotional and callous criticism can have potentially devastating long term consequences, not just for the initial recipient, but for other individuals who may wonder if they will be the next victim. It is better to recognize when your emotional trigger has been activated and wait to calm down and constructively organize your thoughts. The recipient's state of mind is equally important. Even if you, as the giver, are feeling okay, it is important to assess the recipient. In order for the criticism to be productive and constructive, it must be received in the context of a helping spirit and not obscured by emotional obstacles. Before giving criticism ask yourself, "Given what I know about this person and the situation, would I want to be the recipient of what I have to say?"

It is very difficult to gage the psychological receptivity of another human being. Individuals may respond well in one context or situation but reject it in another. It may be that the environment is not right or it may be that the employee is different on this occasion. This can be similar to the proverb that states *"you can never put your foot in the same stream twice."* The stream is different than when you first put your foot in it—the water that was there is long gone down the stream—and the person is different, as they have already experienced having their foot in a stream—it is no longer new. We seldom know

Constructing Criticism

what else might be going on in the life and mind of another. You may offer similar positive and productive criticism as you've done before; however, the recipient may react much differently, not as much to your comments, but because they are psychologically unprepared, dealing with a difficult life event, or a host of other possibilities. Ultimately, you can only do your best to gage the recipient's psychological receptivity and ensure that the location, time, and place are as optimal as possible to realizing your goal of effective, productive, and constructive criticism. Sensitivity, respect, and clarity of thought and purpose are your best allies.

Psychologically, people need to know that they have worth and value. Even though you are criticizing them for a particular issue, they likely do many things well and that should not be neglected in the process. The goal is to effectively communicate the criticism without psychologically crippling the recipient. Criticize without crushing.

6. Evaluate the Criteria Being Used to Validate the Criticism

What is normal or correct in one circumstance may be aberrant in another. Criticism is always offered in context and recipients expect to know what criteria are being used to judge their behavior. We can be expected to follow the rules, as long as we know what those rules—and the consequences for violating them—are. Arbitrary and capricious dictates do not allow individuals to consistently know what is expected. Policies, rules, procedures, guidelines—even social mores—can be identified to support and validate criticism. Recipients deserve to know what yardstick is being used to support the criticism and have the understanding that the yardstick is not "rubber"—bending, twisting, stretching, and changing with every circumstance. Years ago, I had a sign on my desk that read *"Unless you can tell me how you want it done differently, you are just complaining."* This was a constant reminder for me (and others who came to my office) that we all need to consider the validity of our criteria and the potential changes or corrections that might be necessary before our offering our criticism.

"Criticism is the disapproval of people, not for having faults, but having faults different from your own." ~ Unknown

---

7. Visualize the Encounter

Think about the goal, think about your approach, and consider what the recipient is likely to think and do—and be prepared. Always keep the end game in mind, the ultimate goal of the criticism interaction. Is the ultimate goal to have a test of wills or a shooting match? Or, is the ultimate goal to help someone improve so they may do better (G.R.I.P.E.)? Visualize, in your mind's eye, how you would like to see the outcome of this interaction and work to see that you get there. As Steven Covey writes in his book *The 7 Habits of Highly Effective People*, "begin with the end in mind." Know how you want the meeting to turn out and prepare yourself to have the greatest probability of success.

It is important not to just give this encounter some inconsequential thought. Rather, research has demonstrated that actually visualizing the encounter and possible scenarios can be very useful. This process gets you thinking about how best to offer the criticism and it can actually build your confidence in

Constructing Criticism

the delivery. Additionally, as you reflect on your approach, you should also consider issues such as these and how you will handle them:

- What will you do if the person becomes overly defensive? (Think about it now, before you offer the criticism.)
- What if they deny the basis of the criticism? (Do you have clear evidence and information?)
- What if they tell you that your facts are wrong? (Are you dealing with facts or conclusions?)
- What if they become overly emotional?
- What if they ask what "policy" they violated?
- What if they refuse to talk or seemingly listen?
- What if they storm out in a huff?
- What if they become abusive?

Topics such as these must be considered *before* you actually begin to offer criticism. Of course, you will notice that these are all negatively toned; however, *these* are the types of issues with which those of us who offer criticism are most concerned. Do not neglect to consider other possible scenarios. For example, what if they say, "You are right, I should have handled that differently." What will be your reply? Interestingly, in a recent study[5] involving top tier managers, most indicated that they were so concerned with the potential negative consequences, that they gave short shrift to the more positive reactions. It is important, however, to be prepared to accept this acknowledgement and move directly into your discussion on how to make things better; thus, demonstrating to the recipient that your true goal is to help them do better: grow, recover, improve, prosper, or excel. Occasionally, the person offering the criticism is so relieved that the recipient has initially agreed with the criticism and is not offering an unreasonable defense, they almost subconsciously replay the criticism, describing it repetitively. (It is as if we are wondering if they actually *heard* us, so we must need to repeat it; after all we are *criticizing* them!) This course of action is not productive. It is much better to offer your comments, be cognizant that you have seemingly been effective in your communications, and move on. Do not let the euphoria of experiencing criticism success torpedo the goal of your efforts.

8. Organize Your Thoughts

Even after going through the process of visualizing how you would like for the criticism encounter to unfold, you may want to more formally organize your thoughts or the sequence of events that you would like to discuss. You might even wish to make and refer to notes or note cards. This can be useful, as it ensures you get the information correct and can offer an indication that you are organized and have carefully considered your comments. The danger of a less organized approach is that you might inadvertently get off track, off target, and muddle your clarity—or worse. You may start well by discussing the carefully considered issue, but if you launch into a discussion of their religion, family, politics, and so forth you are traveling down a dangerous road. Legal experts in the human resource area have indicated that one of the major mistakes that supervisors can make is to begin addressing issues or make wayward comments that are not germane to the topic of the criticism. It is by far better to be focused, prepared, and organized.

9. Send a Clear Message

Be precise in your language and suggestions or recommendations for change. If you have properly prepared, there should be little ambiguity as to the point and validity of your criticism. Moreover, there should be little mystery as to what it will take to resolve the issue. As indicated in Chapter 4, carefully selecting the right words is extraordinarily important. Even seemingly insignificant word choices can have a dramatic impact. Several years ago, I replicated a study similar to one conducted by psychologist Elizabeth Loftus,[6] that addressed subtle influences in question wording. The study involved different groups of individuals who all watch the same video of an automobile accident. In one group they were asked "How fast were the cars going when they *hit* each other?" With the other group, the question was "How fast were the cars going when they *smashed* each other?" Though the questions were identical except for a single word, there were dramatic differences. Those asked the question with the word "smashed" gave a significantly higher estimate of speed than those who were asked the same question using the word "hit." A single word change had a powerful influence.

Now, as Paul Harvey would say, here is the rest of the story—it gets even better! A few weeks after this phase of the study we had the participants return and asked them a few additional questions. One question asked to all groups was "In the video of the automobile accident that you recently watched, do you remember seeing broken glass?" Again, keep in mind that everyone actually saw the same video—there were no differences in the accident depiction. What was interesting was that those who were previously asked about the speed of the cars with the question involving the word "smashed" remembered seeing broken glass significantly more than those who saw the same video but were asked about the speed using the question with the word "hit." What was even more amazing—there was *no* broken glass in the video. A single word choice in an otherwise similar question not only impacted an estimate of speed, it caused individuals to misremember actual events. Word selection—even those that are seemingly innocuous—can have consequential results.

In many organizations performance evaluations often involve ratings that are worded as: "Exceeds Expectations/Standards," "Meets Expectations/Standards" or is "Below Expectations/Standards." (As an aside, this is not a particularly strong tool as it provides little descriptive variance.) However, if you were to meet with a new employee there could be a tremendous difference in the way such evaluative information is communicated depending on your choice of word or phrase. Psychologically, a comment such as "your work is below expectations" would likely be viewed as being much more critical than the statement "your work is not quite up to expectations"—even if it essentially communicates the same message content. Of course, the work standard is still unmet and the actual rating has not changed; however, the *way* in which the information is discussed can make a dramatic difference from the perspective of the employee. Similarly, if you are providing feedback on how well an individual did on a 10-item exam, for example, a comment such as "you got seven right!" would likely be viewed as more positive than would "you missed three." Although the number of correct items didn't change, the tone of the communication is seemingly much different. Carefully selecting the correct phrase (see more on

Constructing Criticism

this in Chapter 4) and providing clarity of thought in your message is crucial. Additionally, once you are certain that you have effectively communicated and have been understood, do not become repetitive. Make your point and move on. As mentioned above, sometimes critics will seemingly hammer their subject over and over—possibly because they are not sure if they have gotten through or simply because of nervousness or to address awkward pauses. Don't clutter the simplicity of a clear message with needless chatter.

10. Think Win-Win

A Win-Win agreement solidifies your desire to be a helpful and productive force in the life of another. Before giving criticism consider how the solution can be beneficial to everyone involved. The goal is not to have a winner and a loser, but to have a mutual understanding about the topic and how things can change for the better. In criticism-prone circumstances there is really no such thing as Win-Lose. From my perspective, this is really equivalent to a Lose-Lose. Nobody gains unless the goal is to strive for mutual improvement, mutual understanding, and is centered with mutual respect. Keeping the focus on the issue at hand, its potential impact, and a clearly articulated, workable solution can be a benefit for everyone.

Have the Proper Mindset (*If You Don't Read Anything Else About Giving Criticism to Others...Read This!*)

As has been said many times, ones attitude can determine ones altitude. How high you go up the success ladder often depends on the way you view the world and the mindset with which you approach life and address challenges. Having the proper outlook, attitude, and heart when you approach a criticism-prone situation can make all the difference in the world; it can be that which determines either your success or your failure. Criticism is an emotion-laden event. If you do not approach it with the reverence it deserves you will not likely develop into the valued and respected person in the lives of others that we want you to become—a person of influence who leaves a legacy of respect, understanding, support, and assistance; a person who helps others to Grow, Recover, Improve, Prosper, and Excel. In order to become that person, everything begins with the proper spirit. All of the advice offered in this book will be of little value if you do not approach the difficult task of handling criticism with the right mindset.

As it relates to giving criticism, here is one of the most important points for you to consider. One of the best ways to get into the proper frame of reference for providing criticism to others is to *think about offering criticism as though you were offering it to a young child*—perhaps your child. Ask yourself: Is your goal to psychologically beat up your child? Is your criticism intended to make a child feel bad about themselves? Is it to put them in their place or show them who's the boss? Or, conversely, is it instead to help them to *grow*? It is to help them *recover* from an upset? Is it to help them *improve* and develop into a better person? Is it to help them *prosper* and flourish? Is it to help them *excel* in all that they strive to achieve? How do you want others to treat your child? How do you want to treat your child? This is the proper starting mindset when considering the best way to offer criticism. Your goal should be to strive to help, not hurt; to comfort not cripple.

In a similar way, this same mindset helps us to consider the Win-Lose problem. Considering the approach

Constructing Criticism

of offering criticism to a child (metaphorically or otherwise) can help us to better orient our thinking. Is your goal to *win* by providing crippling, destructive, disparaging comments...and have your child *lose*? Is your real purpose to show your young child that you are better than they are? Are you really trying to prove that you are stronger than your child? Let's hope not. It is far better to operate from a position where your goal is to have a Win-Win result. Your child wins by learning, growing, improving, and so forth; and you win by nurturing a spirit and helping another to become the type of person that you know they can. As others have often said about success in many areas of life—it's all in the approach. (Also true when successfully landing an airplane; the quality of the landing is often dependent on the quality of the approach.)

To be clear, when I propose this mindset for offering criticism to a child, I am not saying that you should talk to them as though they *are* a child—that would be disrespectful and demeaning. It is not about your *manner* of communication, it is about your *attitude* toward the communication. It is about how you psychologically frame your approach to providing criticism to others in order to become a person of positive influence in their lives.

"Treat a man as he appears to be, and you make him worse. But treat a man as if he already were what he potentially could be, and you make him what he should be."
~ Goethe

Moving Forward

As we consider these 10 points before offering criticism and having the proper criticism mindset, it is important to highlight that all of this occurs *before* you utter a single word. No shooting from the hip or winging it here. Productive and constructive criticism that helps others to G.R.I.P.E. requires thoughtful effort and contemplation. The Criticism Action Plan found in the appendix may be helpful as you consider how best to approach giving criticism. Clearly this is not the most economical process that is available and it takes a great deal of discipline and work; however, the positive effects this can have on the economy of the human spirit and individual interactions are immeasurable.

In addition to the critical mindset offered above, it might also be helpful to think about preparing to offer criticism as if it were a formal meeting. Do you want the meeting conducted by someone who is unprepared, maybe jotting down a few last minute notes seconds before arriving, or do you want someone who has done their homework and is organized? Similarly, do you want to attend an important college class conducted by a professor who only glances at the material as they walk through the classroom door with no other real preparation? Just as an improvised meeting or unprepared class is not as likely to be valuable, criticism that is not well thought out may be much less productive. Similarly, if I am scheduled to give a lecture or presentation, I carefully think about my topic and my audience. Why am I there? Who is my audience? What am I going to say to get them motivated? How am I going to grab their attention? How am I going to best explain the information? How will we interact? How will I formulate an effective closing message? How will I make a positive contribution to their lives? Dealing with criticism is no less important.

Chapter 7
Criticism: The Gift of Giving

"Criticism, like rain, should be gentle enough to nourish a man's growth without destroying his roots." ~ *Frank A. Clark*

When Giving Criticism
After the Criticism
Having the Criticism Conversation

When *Giving* Criticism

Everything that we have addressed up until now is essentially occurring behind the eyes and between the ears of the person who is planning to offer criticism. If we have followed the path that has been outlined, we have yet to utter a critical word; however, we are now prepared to actually *give* the criticism we have carefully planned. As with our preparation before giving criticism, there are helpful tips to consider when we begin moving toward actually communicating the criticism information. In many ways the ideas and suggestions offered in this chapter flow from the previous one. Some of the distinctions in what to consider before and during the presentation of criticism can be a bit arbitrary and could actually fit in either place. The point, however, is to actually consider *all* of these points so as to have the best chance of providing criticism that is productive, constructive, and does not elicit the defensiveness that devastates effective criticism communication.

1. Don't Procrastinate

Once all of the important points have been considered *before* giving criticism, and you have concluded that it's appropriate to proceed, do not procrastinate. Don't put off giving criticism because you think it is unpleasant, especially in the workplace where you are responsible for supervising others. As discussed previously, most of us want to be the "good guy" and rendering criticism reminds us that we cannot always be in the position to offer praise. While it is certainly true that being overly critical is far from wise, avoiding criticism for fear of creating a confrontation can be worse. Procrastination seldom makes things better. Imagine taking a carton of milk from the fridge and realizing that it has gone sour. If you set the carton on the counter and come back a day or two later to see if it might have gotten better—trust me, it won't be. Conversely, procrastination may cause circumstances to get much worse, lacking the attention that is needed. Further, if you are a supervisor charged with the responsibility to effectively manage others, failing to offer accurate and productive criticism is tantamount to job neglect. Consider the role of a Field Training Officer (FTO) in a police department.[1] These are the individuals that provide experience-based training for new police officers in the field. The job of a police officer is difficult and demanding; we want those in police service to be well equipped to handle this task. It is the FTO's responsibility to provide training, criticism, and direction. Imagine the consequences of an FTO who procrastinated in providing the new officer with much needed criticism. Depending on the situation, such a delay could result in a tragic outcome—especially if the criticism involved issues of officer safety in dealing with dangerous circumstances.

Criticism: The Gift of Giving

To be clear, I am not talking about a short delay until cooler heads and emotions prevail, as was discussed in the previous chapter. It would make no sense to launch into a criticism dialogue when the parties are emotionally, psychological, or physically spent. Here I am more specifically referring to the tendency to delay addressing important issues that need attention even after determining that productive and constructive criticism is appropriate.

2. Maintain R-E-S-P-E-C-T (The Aretha Rule)

Aretha Franklin had it right with the title of her signature song, when dealing with criticism it is important that we maintain R-E-S-P-E-C-T—even when it is difficult. People have different worldviews, different perspectives, different values, and so forth. People will often see the world in diverse ways. Someone once told me that respect is like air; if you take it away that is the *only* thing people will think about. The term *"respect"* derives from the Latin *"re"* meaning back, and *"specere,"* looking back; it literally means *"to look back at, regard, or consider."* In this way, to respect another is to consider their views; to have regard for how they may be interpreting events. In fact, when you move away from respect, you are often eliciting the very thing you are otherwise striving to avoid: defensiveness. When people feel that their personal character is being assaulted, the original topic of the criticism conversation is pushed aside. Now the focus will be on defending their integrity or reputation.

"The actual criticism occurs in the mind of another" ~ *Dawson Garrett*

When taking classes in seminary, I was taught the prayer "Lord, please help me forgive those who sin differently than me." If you provide a common perspective, that we all have weaknesses, quirks, and differences, we can focus less on those personal traits and more on respecting (though not necessarily agreeing with) the differences. You can maintain a sense of respect toward another even if you disagree with their view or position.

3. Be Accountable and Responsible

To be accountable means that you assume appropriate responsibility for how the criticism is delivered. This involves all of the elements discussed in this and the previous chapters. You are working to ensure the best possible result in the criticism you offer to others. Interestingly, the word "responsible" separates in to *"response"* and *"able;"* literally you are *able* to *respond.* You should hold yourself accountable to generate all of the information and facts that are needed to assess the validity and appropriateness of offering the criticism and be responsible for delivering the criticism in a manner that reduces defensive reactions and provides others with the opportunity to G.R.I.P.E.

"Speak when you're angry—and you will make the best speech you'll ever regret."
~ Laurence J. Peter

When you deal with topics as sensitive as criticism, you can't really fake it. If you are going though the steps because you have been told to or because you are "supposed to," then you are likely to be much

Criticism: The Gift of Giving

less effective. People tend to havé great "sincerity radars"—they can tell when you are doing something that is not in your heart. The old joke is "sincerity...oh I can fake that!" The reality is—not so much. In emotionally heightened, criticism-prone situations, your true character and motivation will likely be revealed and detected. You have to approach this difficult issue with an authentic nature. You must have a true desire to become a better individual that truly wants to help others; otherwise your insincerity will leak out. Such is the nature of emotions.

4. Remain Calm – Monitor Your Own Emotions

Obviously, giving criticism can be emotionally taxing and psychologically demanding. Physiological cues such as increasing pulse rate, a feeling of flushness, clenching muscles—especially in the face and jaw—can alert you that your emotions are on the rise. This may be due to your own apprehension about giving criticism or it may be the result of behavior from the recipient. Either way, the goal is to keep your own emotions in check.

Focus intently on keeping a calm, steady tone and demeanor. The best antidote for increased emotionality is to continually remind yourself that you are providing beneficial information that is intended to help the person G.R.I.P.E. Actually, if you have developed a trust relationship with the recipient and have followed the steps that have been outlined, it is likely that the criticism interaction will be much less eventful than you might have imagined. Once the recipient can see that you truly do have their interests at heart, that you are not trying to intentionally crush their self-esteem, that you have carefully considered your comments, and that you are offering the information in a spirit of improvement, their defensive shields will tend to go down.

On those occasions where you do feel your tensions uncomfortably rising or your collar getting hot, consider a strategy to introduce a *pause* in the conversation. A pause allows you to both re-center your emotions and may provide a brief distraction from the tension. This pause could be a short break or even consist of a prearranged signal, interruption, or phone call from another person. One thing I have done if things are getting heated, especially in cases where the other party is engaging in an emotional venting exercise, is to politely interrupt and say "excuse me just a minute." (Depending on the circumstance, in addition to the polite verbal interruption, I will sometimes briefly hold up my hand to *visually* signal my pause request.) I then open my desk drawer, pull out a 3 by 5 laminated card and take a moment to read it. I start to return it to my drawer, but then pause again to briefly re-read it. I then return the card to the desk, close the drawer, and say something like "I'm sorry, please continue," or I might say "Thank you, OK, how about if we focus on ..." Interestingly, this little tactic accomplishes two things: first, it allows for a needed pause to short-circuit the escalating emotionality, and second, it further creates a psychological break as the person is now devoting some of their cognitive attention to wondering what I am doing, what is on that card, and trying to figure out what it all might mean. Meanwhile, we have injected this much needed break to bring the discussion back on track. Although this may not always work, it is something that I have used successfully when dealing with upset individuals in a variety of situations. (By the way, the laminated card in my desk was given to me at a leadership confer-

Criticism: The Gift of Giving

ence and has a Latin phrase that roughly translates as: "Don't let the illegitimate offspring win" or some variation of that theme). Of course, it doesn't really matter what, if anything, is on the card, as it is the action of consulting this "mysterious" document that provides the relief. I once used the approach with an attorney who was becoming increasingly irritated in our discussion. After I engaged this pause technique and put the card back in the desk, it was clear that I had interrupted his verbal assault plan and emotions were slightly less tense. Weeks later I saw the same attorney who greeted me cordially. After a bit of small talk, he said "A few weeks ago during our meeting (he called it a *meeting*) you took out some card and looked at it while we were talking. You know…after you did that, almost all I could think about was what the heck was on that card!" Mission accomplished.

5. Stick to the Facts and Be Specific

Be precise and have specific details as to what is or is not working. Although we discussed these important elements in the previous chapter, their importance cannot be over estimated. Facts are not conclusions. Facts are not judgments. Facts focus on the *what* not the *why*. Now that you are actually giving criticism you must stay on course. If you are not completely sure of the facts, you are not prepared to offer productive and constructive criticism. Make sure you fully understand the problem, the facts, and the yardstick against which you are measuring the behavior. Criticism communications can be the most emotionally charged and difficult in the communication process, so choose your manner and words carefully. Every word is consequential in criticism communications. People are likely already on edge and the emotional cloud may cause perceptual distortions as they filter the information that they are being presented. Unfortunately some people tend to clutter an otherwise clear message with excessive verbiage, especially when nervous or when encountering longer-than-comfortable conversational pauses. Resist the temptation to over dramatize, over explain, or over state the criticism. Clearly communicated criticism that is supported by facts—not emotion, conjecture, or inference—is the best criticism communication mode.

General comments or pejorative statements are not going to be productive. Specificity in your observations, your facts, and, if appropriate, your suggestions is critical. If you say to me that my work is "sloppy," "messy," "not cutting it," "not up to par," or any of dozens of other less-than-clear terms you will not be giving me the needed direction and guidance. Your comments should not require me to guess as to what you actually mean. If my report is "not cutting it," I don't know if that means you don't like my style, if you think my grammar is problematic, you dislike my penmanship, or if I am putting information in the wrong blanks. As the person offering the criticism designed to help me to G.R.I.P.E., you must be accountable for providing clear, fact-based information designed to help me improve.

6. Criticize the Deed, Not the Doer

When offering criticism that is intended to be productive and constructive your focus is on the action not the actor; it is criticism of the performance, not the performer. The goal is to provide the recipient with information that will help them to grow, recover, improve, prosper, or excel. The goal is not to assail the self-esteem of the one receiving the criticism. If you find yourself slipping into criticism that focuses on the individual rather than the behavior, you have missed your goal. Focusing on the action, deed, or performance rather than the person can help reduce the potential for emotional defensiveness. As mentioned previously, "You" statements, particularly those that are accusatory, can be a problem because they tend to focus the criticism on the individual. "You really made a mess of things!" "You did this all wrong!" "You are a ...!" This places the criticism spotlight back on the person, not the actual behavior. It can help to primarily use "you" statements for positives such as, "You really did a great job!" or "You are doing very well!" If you are addressing a concern or criticism, it is often better to phrase it from *your* perspective with "I" statements, such as "I am concerned that..." or "I worried that...." You then follow that with the fact-based specifics that focus on the behavior.

"Kindness is more important than wisdom, and the recognition of this is the beginning of wisdom." ~ *Theodore Isaac Rubin, M.D.*

---

7. Make Sure It's a Dialogue

The goal of criticism communication is to ensure that there is a dialogue, not a monologue. Management practices of the past tended to focus on control and blame. They engaged in the "I Talk – You Listen" monologue mode. However, if you do not allow for a two-way dialogue, you may miss important information that might help you better assess the particulars of the situation. You should encourage the recipient to get engaged in the conversation. They will feel better about being heard (assuming you have practiced your active listening skills) even if they may not like the message. Additionally, you may learn new information that could impact your views and provide a more complete story or picture of the situation. Keep the discourse open and consider the possibility that you might learn that the recipient may have had a plausible reason for the action that you are criticizing, a tidbit of information that would be undisclosed if operating from the monologue mode. Such a situation could leave the recipient feeling upset, sensing things are unjust, and certainly unheard, not a sound combo for effective communication. One great technique that I consistently use to ensure a better chance for a two-way interaction is to ask questions (see Chapter 4). For example, after tentatively providing my factual observations and understanding of the situation, I will end with something like "Is that correct, or am I missing something?" or "Do I have that right or is there other information that should be considered?" When I ask questions I *automatically* begin the process of creating a dialogue. Asking questions signals that you are interested and concerned; it lets the other person know that you are open for discussion and reduces defensiveness.

8. Be Prepared for a Variety of Responses

In the previous chapter you considered the likely scenarios that may occur as you prepared for criticism-prone situations. We also discussed that criticism received well in one context may result in an emotional meltdown in another. As a result, when actually delivering criticism, you must be as prepared as possible for the reality of these reactions. Keeping alert to the emotionality and resonance of the conversation is important so that you will know how to best handle it. Here you will implement the plan that you have previously considered, based on

Criticism: The Gift of Giving

the actual observed response to your criticism. You cannot always predict how people will respond, even if you are basing your predications on past interactions. Situational factors may influence people to behave in ways that may not be consistent with their usual demeanor. You may not know if a contributing factor to the behavior that you are addressing or if an unexpected response to your criticism is at least partially rooted in a personal struggle (e.g., fatigue from working overtime or going to school), family predicament (e.g., sick child, marriage difficulties), or other situational influences. The point is to be as prepared as possible for all reasonable eventualities.

9. Ensure Effective Communication has Occurred

This bit of advice is easier said than done; however, the goal is to avoid any misunderstandings concerning the topic of the criticism or the resolution. In this regard, remember that feedback is extremely important. According to Ken Blanchard, "feedback is the breakfast of champions." As you will recall from our communication model, feedback is a critical link to ensure that the recipient has an accurate rendering of the message intended by the sender. You will want to use a feedback technique to elicit from the recipient their understanding of the criticism. However, a simple closed-ended question such as "Do you understand?" is not a good feedback tool. Such a "yes or no" approach almost ensures that the recipient will indicate agreement in order to keep from being seen as inattentive or unintelligent. Some people find saying something like the following to be helpful: "OK, we've talked about a number of things, let's compare notes to make sure we are on the same page." The goal is to make sure that nothing important is missed, misunderstood, or misinterpreted. At that point you ask the recipient to work with you in expressing the gist of the conversation and any agreed upon action. The feedback technique must be something that is comfortable for both you and the recipient. However, asking a recipient to "Repeat everything I've told you to be sure you've got it right" is both condescending and likely to elicit increased anxiety. Unfortunately, more than one leadership text suggests that potentially ill-fated approach. It is much better to keep this as a reciprocal effort, reinforcing the goal of productive and constructive criticism communication.

10. Focus on the Future Not the Past

Direct your attention to things that can be done to fix problems that lie ahead. The problem of the past has already occurred; the goal is not to dwell on the past issue, but to use it as a tool to prevent similar occurrences in the future. Destructive criticism is directed at "punishing" the recipient for past actions. Productive and constructive criticism is future oriented. Punishment is past oriented; it informs us that what we have done may not be acceptable, but offers no guidance on how to do things differently in the future. The higher purpose it not to affix blame; it is to effect positive change. Of course, the typical criticism conversation is based on some past occurrence or event. However, what we are addressing here is your response to that past event; suggesting that it be less about what has already happened and more about how to correctly move forward. Look through the metaphorical windshield to see what is ahead rather than focus on the rear-view mirror. Too much attention to what you have already passed—rather than what's ahead—is a recipe for disaster.

Criticism: The Gift of Giving

11. Be Concrete Regarding Purpose and Expectations

Don't require people to guess as to how they can improve. Don't play traffic cop, "Do you know why I pulled you over?" or the Boss version, "Do you know why I called you in?" Your goal is to be clear in purpose, communication, and expectation. However, as mentioned above, the problem with punishment is that it often reprimands the recipient for something they did wrong without regard for explaining how things should be done differently in the future. For example, consider this exchange:

Boss: "You are constantly turning in work that is not up to par, I'm going to have to write you up."

Recipient: "I'm not sure what you mean?"

Boss: "It's not my responsibility to do your job; if you don't know how to write a decent report you shouldn't be working here!"

Or:

Parent: "Your room is a pigsty!"

Child: "What do you mean?"

Parent: "You know what I mean, I don't need to say another word!"

Or:

Teacher: "This report is a mess."

Student: "What's wrong with it?"

Teacher: "You should know what's wrong. Fix it!"

Here we have terrible criticism that is unfocused, unclear, and obviously not productive. In the first example it's centered on some vague statement about not being up to par (whatever that means…assuming it is not about your golf game) and offers no glimmer of a suggestion for improvement. To indicate that something is a "mess" but offer no other information or specific expectations for improvement is not communicating a helping attitude. In these cases we essentially have all punishment and no constructive suggestions as to how to do better. This is not the type of criticism that helps people to G.R.I.P.E. If you have determined that offering criticism is appropriate, you must be prepared with specific suggestions for improvement; you must communicate exactly what "success" looks like in whatever endeavor you are discussing.

12. Acknowledge Criticism Occurs in Context: It Can Be Subjective

Just as we must acknowledge our own contributions in certain circumstances when providing criticism to others, it is best to acknowledge that the criticism can certainly be subjective depending on the context. In some cases criticism may be offered as a result of a difference in philosophy or style. It may be the result of divergence in addressing certain issues rather than a dichotomous black or white, right or wrong distinction. The world does not always operate in an either-or fashion. In fact, it may be the result of a particular policy or procedure, for example, which could be completely contradicted in another context. If you don't think context matters consider the following. Assume you are a TV producer meeting with network executives in Hollywood and you are discussing shooting a pilot. Now imagine you are going through airport security and you begin discussing shooting a pilot. Same words; different context. I wouldn't want to be standing anywhere around you at the airport. Context matters! Whatever the case, criticism is often subjective and providing that acknowledgement to the recipient may help to protect their self-esteem by allowing them to recognize that the criticism is about some action in *this* situation, not about their worth in general.

"Be not angry that you cannot make **others** *as you wish them to be; since you cannot make* **yourself** *as you wish to be."*
~ *Thomas a' Kempis*

After the Criticism

The goal of providing productive and constructive criticism does not end with the conclusion of the criticism conversation. Offering criticism is a process that continues well after the initial dialogue. If you are truly focused on helping another to grow, recover, improve, prosper, or excel, what you do *after* delivering criticism is as important as any of the other phases we have discussed. If you really want to be a positive influence in the life of the recipient, you must do more than *say* you are willing to help, you must *show* them as evidenced by the action of your conviction. People are judged far more by what they do than what they say. In this case you are being judged on your ability to offer criticism as we have redefined it.

1. Be Positive

The goal of P.C. Criticism is to help, not harm; so you may wish to consider ways to thank them for their past accomplishments and let them know you look forward to working with them to accomplish the objective you have mutually agreed upon. Expectations often breed the anticipated results, what psychologists call a self-fulfilling prophesy. If we expect others to improve we may likely see that improvement because we treat the recipient with respect and encouragement and they reciprocate with results. The goal is to reflect an attitude that the other person *will* succeed.

2. Be Accessible

If the desire is to help, you must be approachable when questions or concerns arise. Too often bad critics spew their less-than-productive advice and then retire to the seclusion of their offices—so as not to be bothered with the unsavory aftermath of the mess they have created. Conversely, P.C. critics want to be available to keep the recipient on course and give direction and guidance as needed. Again, the goal of criticism is not to just effectively deliver it and leave the recipient floundering for support. The aspiration of the P.C. critic is to help that person G.R.I.P.E.

3. Be Patient

It may be that the criticism has struck a sensitive nerve or exposed the recipient to a realization that they may not be as prepared for the task or situation as they first thought. The recipient may need some time to reflect and digest the criticism. Patience does not always work, but impatience almost never does.

4. Follow-up

Helpful follow-up is not unstructured; it is planned, focused, intentional, and directed. In order to be the most effective P.C. critic, you must do more than have a positive attitude and be accessible; you must seek out the recipient and engage in goal-checking and follow-up. When you work with another after offering criticism, you are

Criticism: The Gift of Giving

communicating to that individual that they are a person of worth and you have a stake in their success. To be meaningful, follow-up should be more than asking someone "How's it going?" As we all know, this will likely result in the usual automatic response. As an alternate for the automatic exchange described above, consider offering something such as "How about you and I meet before the end of the week to go over what we discussed the other day." Make the offer, keep the commitment, and provide the recipient quality feedback on their progress. This level of attention and concern likely will engender a strong, positive regard for you from the recipient—allowing you to become an affirming and appreciated influence in their life.

"A pat on the back is only a few vertebrae removed from a kick in the pants, but miles ahead in results." ~ *Ella W. Wilcox*

Having the Criticism Conversation

This is something that you must consider from the onset. There is always a pattern or flow to a conversation, and much of that depends on the participants. You must consider how you will begin and end the criticism conversation in a way that does not significantly exceed your comfort zone. Venturing too far afield from your comfort level can create unneeded stress and tension. Delivering criticism is already a challenging proposition; there is no reason to make it more cumbersome by trying to be something that you are not. People who try to break the tension with humor, for example, but who are not particularly good at humor, can create unintended consequences. The recipient might even perceive that the critic is flippant, not taking the issue seriously, or worse, is making light of them.

It might be helpful to start the conversation with a clear indication of why you wanted to meet with the individual. Frequently, communication experts talk of a sandwich approach to offering criticism. This is something along the lines of telling the recipient, "you are generally OK, *but* you do this wrong; however, I still like you." (And recall our discussion on the use of words like "but" and "however" in a previous chapter.) I am not a fan of creating false praise or offering feigned compliments. In a criticism-prone environment where tension and emotions can run high, offering an opening observation with accurate feedback can help to assure the individual that they remain a person of worth. Realize, though, that some recipients will simply gloss over the compliment, waiting for the other metaphorical shoe to drop—waiting to get down to the real business of the criticism. Particularly in circumstances where it is obvious that dispensing criticism is the purpose of the encounter, many people report they would prefer to get right to the point rather than engage in idle chatter.

As we all know, a conversation has a beginning, middle, and end. Your goal is to make sure that you clearly communicate criticism in a way that allows the recipient to use it to their benefit in a respectful, succinct, and thoughtful manner that does not unduly assail their self-esteem. Once that is accomplished, make certain that you have an "exit strategy" to conclude the conversation. You will want to bring the conversation to a close so as not to overextend the processing capacity of either party (our minds can handle only so much) or to create an opportunity for endless debate. The best approach is to have a plan for concluding the discussion. Keep in mind, however, that even once the discussion is over, the *process* of giving criticism continues as you consider how best to offer follow-up and support.

In the chapter that follows we are going to go through a step-by-step process in delivering productive and constructive criticism. This is where we begin to "put it all together." All of the ideas and suggestions that we have addressed thus far should be considered as you engage the criticism conversation.

Chapter 8
Putting It All Together: The Criticism Conversation

"Criticism must be given with respect to be valued." ~ Brady James

We have examined a great deal of information on how best to consider and provide criticism. Clearly this is no task for a lightweight. Giving productive and constructive criticism is not easy; it requires thoughtful reflection and a caring spirit. Unfortunately, all too often it is offered as an emotional reaction with little thought or deliberation. Clearly one of the biggest obstacles to giving (and receiving) criticism is overcoming defensive emotions. The critic, however, often has the ability to mitigate defensive reactions. The choice of words and phrases, the manner of tone and expression, the approaching mindset, the method of delivery, the consideration of attributional and cognitive biases, the willingness to blunt our own emotional response (the Criticism Corridor) and construct a more complete story (the Paul Harvey Solution), and our decision to carefully weigh the necessity, form, and function of our criticism (the Aretha Rule) can have a dramatic impact. All of the information that we have considered in the preceding chapters must now be collectively brought together in the criticism conversation. Having properly weighed the prerequisites for offering criticism, it's now time to have the discussion.

In the section that follows are some suggestions for how you might want to approach the task of giving criticism. These are mere suggestions and you must develop a style and delivery that best suits your own personality. What we have discussed in the previous chapters address various issues in thinking about and delivering criticism. Here I will offer a few steps for your consideration when you are actually having the criticism conversation. You have already considered the merits of offering criticism and have reviewed all of the various issues related to providing productive and constructive criticism. Now we will more specifically consider how you might approach the actual dialogue. In the sequence and steps below, I will "construct" a criticism conversation. I will be adding to the conversation with successive steps. Keep in mind that this is done to help you improve your own form and style. Once you develop the confidence to better handle criticism-prone circumstances, your delivery will become much more seamless. The steps are offered merely to highlight important issues that should be considered in developing the overall criticism dialogue.

Step 1. Consider and Reconsider

OK—so I'm not necessarily going for overkill; however, making sure you have considered *everything* we have previously discussed is critical (root of criticism). You must be sure that offering criticism is appropriate, that you've identified the actual problem or issue, that you've assessed the fact-based criteria involved, and you have fully considered the desired outcome and how best to get there. You must rededicate your commitment to working to offer criticism as a means to help others G.R.I.P.E. You must consider all of the situational, psychological, and strategic issues provided in the previous chapters. If you do not have a solid foundation, the criticism you construct will be much less sturdy.

Step 2. Offer a Greeting—Then Get to the Point

It's fine to offer a genuine greeting; in fact, depending on the circumstance and your personal relationship with the other person this may go a long way to disarm some apprehension. You should always begin from a position of respect and a part of that respect is for the time and consideration of others. Excessive small talk is likely less productive or welcome and may even come across as disingenuous. You may really want to engage in small talk to dissipate your *own* discomfort; however, it may be viewed as little more than chatter or noise. Depending on the situation, the recipient may know that something is amiss and may not really be listening to or appreciate excessive chatter. Without being exceedingly abrupt, it is often best to get to the point of your discussion.

Example: *"Hi Chris. It is good to see you. ... Chris, the reason I wanted to visit with you is to discuss the situation that has developed with the attendance policy..."*

Notice at this introductory point we are talking about a very general policy, not any specific accusation.

Step 3. Provisionally Present the Problem or Predicament

Based on facts and direct observation or evidence, carefully state the problem or issue as you see it. This is where word choice, phrasing, and less deterministic language discussed in the previous chapters become important. The goal is to objectively present the information without judgment or blame—stick with the facts and all of the relevant information that you have gathered. Remember part of this process is to better understand the entire circumstance and, if possible, gain information.

Example: *"Hi Chris. It is good to see you. ... Chris, the reason I wanted to visit with you is to discuss the situation that has developed with the attendance policy. As I understand it, you have reported late to work at least 3 times in the last month."*

You might note there is a "you" statement here; however in this case it not the negatively steeped directive approach such as "You should..." "You always...." "You never..." Here we are merely identifying the specifics based on the facts as we understand them as to *who* did *what*—vital elements for an effective conversation.

Step 4. Offer an Interim Understanding of These Facts

After tentatively stating the situation as you currently see it, you may wish to cautiously address your *interim* understanding of the information you have just presented. The use of the word "interim" is intentional as it connotes a provisional or potentially temporary understanding. Psychologically, it suggests that you have not yet reached a full conclusion. You want to be clear in your discussion as to how you reached your interim understanding and how the facts relate. You should likely discuss the impact of the behavior so as to substantiate the reason you are having the conversation. As we continue to construct the conversation in the example below, the late attendance as well as the impact such behavior has on others is addressed.

Example: *"Hi Chris. It is good to see you. … Chris, the reason I wanted to visit with you is to discuss the situation that has developed with the attendance policy. As I understand it, you have reported late to work at least 3 times in the last month. This seems to suggest that our policy is not being followed. Of course, this is not only a rule violation, it can be a real problem for others who work in the office and have to stay late or cover for people who are not showing up on time."*

If the behavior is seemingly uncharacteristic (for example, they have been a great employee for years and this issue has only recently developed) or if you expect a type of "you think I am totally worthless" thinking (sometimes referred to as the *Chicken Little Effect*—the sky is falling!), you might want to use *anticipatory contrasting*. (This is sometimes called Dialogue Distinctions, as you are distinguishing what you are particularly addressing in the criticism communication from other issues.) Just like a radiologist may inject a patient with a contrasting dye to better differentiate elements on an x-ray, here you contrast or differentiate the present discussion from more general issues—it is essentially an ego-preserving method. You want to clearly communicate that you are currently focusing on this specific issue and not something more globally. You are addressing *this* circumstance; you are not devaluing their overall worth, usual performance, or character. In the modified example below, we are using this approach in anticipation of the Chicken Little Effect on the part of the recipient.

Example: *"Hi Chris. It is good to see you. … Chris, the reason I wanted to visit with you is to discuss the situation that has developed with the attendance policy. <u>I don't want you to think that I am dissatisfied with your overall work; you have been a solid employee for years. I want to</u>*

*address this one issue. As I understand it, you have re-
ported late to work at least 3 times in the last month. This
seems to suggest that our policy is not being followed. Of
course, this is not only a rule violation, it can be a real
problem for others who work in the office and have to stay
late or cover for people who are not showing up on time."*

In this case you have made it clear that your focus is squarely on the expressed behavior not on their
worth more generally. This contrasting or differentiation process can also be used later in the conversation. For example, if you did not address the contrast
earlier and you see that the person is moving toward
the Chicken Little Effect, you can use this approach
to get things back on track.

Example: *"Hi Chris. It is good to see you. ... Chris,
the reason I wanted to visit with you is to discuss the situation that has developed with the attendance policy. As I
understand it, you have reported late to work at least 3
times in the last month. This seems to suggest that our
policy is not being followed. Of course, this is not only a
rule violation, it can be a real problem for others who work
in the office and have to stay late or cover for people who
are not showing up on time."*

Recipient: "Are you saying I'm a bad employee?"

*Response: Not at all. I don't want you to think that
I am dissatisfied with your overall work; you have been
a solid employee for years. I am really only focusing on
this one issue.*

Of course, the response will be guided by the
experience and relationship you have with the individual. Providing such a distinction in the conversation can help to clarify motive, intent, and purpose.
This process also gives others a point of reference for
your comments. For example, I once had a bad experience with a particular hotel. I thought the manager

needed to be aware of the problem; however, I did not want the manager to think that my motivation or intention was to get something from him. I was not looking for an adjustment to my bill or to get a free night, I just wanted to give him some information that could make his hotel better. As a result, I started my conversation like this: "Hi Jim. I had a service issue develop here at the hotel that I think you might want to know about. First, let me start out by telling you that I have stayed at your hotel many times in the past and will be staying here many times in the future. I am not looking to get anything "comped" and I am not trying to get anyone fired; I just want to give you some information that I believe you can use to address a service issue that I think will help you to create a better experience for your guests. Here's what happened…"

Now, you can imagine that hotel managers likely deal with all kinds of people, some of whom are trying to get "something for nothing." By addressing this upfront and letting him know that I didn't want anything other than to give him some information that could potentially allow his hotel to operate more effectively, I eliminated that possible concern and likely allowed him to lower his defensive shields.

Step 5. Concluding Criticism Question

One of the real "secrets" in constructing more effective criticism is to use the fine art of questions. This was more fully discussed in a previous chapter. Now that you have identified the problem or issue, have expressed the facts as you know them, and have offered your interim understanding, it is often a great approach to end with a well-directed question. As mentioned previously, ending your initial dialogue with a question signals that you are open to other information and that you have not already "convicted" the recipient. Asking questions can not only temper defensiveness, it can provide you with an opportunity to get potentially valuable information that could alter your perspective of events. It also automatically begins the process of moving the conversation to a dialogue in which the recipient becomes an active participant. (I wrote an entire book on the significance and power of questions...that's how important I believe this is!)

Example: *"Hi Chris. It is good to see you. ... Chris, the reason I wanted to visit with you is to discuss the situation that has developed with the attendance policy. As I understand it, you have reported late to work at least 3 times in the last month. This seems to suggest that our policy is not being followed. Of course, this is not only a rule violation, it can be a real problem for others who work in the office and have to stay late or cover for people who are not showing up on time. "Is there something going on that I am not aware of?" or "Is this information correct or is there something else?"*

Asking either of the above questions (don't ask both—pick one or, better yet, create one that works for you) gives the recipient the opportunity to accept, dispute, or elaborate on the information presented or the conclusions reached.

Step 6. Listen (Lather; Rinse; Repeat)

Now it's time to practice your *active* listening—which you started by asking a question. Carefully listen to the reply. If you are not completely clear about the response, ask another carefully worded question. As mentioned previously, asking a question not only allows you to gain more information, it helps to keep emotions in better balance by engaging your cognitive functions—your brain power. The recipient might provide you with other information that could shed new light on the situation. For example, the recipient might begin by apologizing and relating that his mother has recently been moved to hospice care and things have been difficult. Wow—talk about a perspective shift. (This also points to the importance of how you create your internal, attributional story discussed in Chapter 5.) As you carefully listen, try your best to analyze the emotional tone and be alert for defensiveness. If appropriate, use your contrasting or differentiation techniques.

Example: *"Hi Chris. It is good to see you. ... Chris, the reason I wanted to visit with you is to discuss the situation that has developed with the attendance policy. As I understand it, you have reported late to work at least 3 times in the last month. This seems to suggest that our policy is not being followed. Of course, this is not only a rule violation, it can be a real problem for others who work in the office and have to stay late or cover for people who are not showing up on time. Is there something going on that I am not aware of?"*

Recipient: "Well actually there is. I was hoping to handle things by myself and keep this private, but the truth is my mother was recently put in hospice care and it has been a very emotional and difficult time in our family. I didn't want to say anything, because I am not looking to offer excuses. I have come in late a few times; things are a bit more difficult with everything that is going on right now. I am sorry I let you down."

This is likely a *huge* shift in your perspective of this situation. Because we easily create a negative attributional story about the character or intentions of another based on incomplete information—this can hit you like a ton of bricks. Of course, the problem and its impact on others is still there; however how you reflect on this new information and respond may be markedly different.

Step 7. Reflect / Respond

Now they have replied—what next? You will have to reflect on the entirety of the information that you have received and determine how best to handle it. Your response can be as varied as the shades of situations you will encounter. For example, you might find the new information requires more consideration, so you may ask to visit with them again later after you have had time to digest it. You might decide this information provides a reasonable explanation for the questioned behavior and nothing more needs to be addressed. You may decide that though they offer a reasonable and understandable response and you now know more about why the behavior occurred, you still need to engage corrective action. You will have to determine the next step based on your previous understanding of the facts, as well as any new information that may have been brought to light.

Now you will move to the next step in the criticism conversation. Given your preparation in considering, developing, and offering the criticism, you will have in your mind an appropriate path or conclusion. Occasionally, a recipient may respond with an emotional reaction or a response that is not clearly related to the criticism you are offering. You may need to redirect the individual to the specific issue you are addressing through a contrasting technique. If they offer a reply that is a version of "everybody is doing that" or "several people do the same thing and no one has said anything about it before," you will need to examine if there are, in fact, such contributions to this situation. You may want to ask clarifying questions designed to elicit actual examples regarding this supposed behavior. You are looking for specifics, not general platitudes. That does not necessarily mean that the criticism is not warranted or that they person should not be accountable; however it may require a different response from you.

Example: *"Hi Chris. It is good to see you. ... Chris, the reason I wanted to visit with you is to discuss the situation that has developed with the attendance policy. As I understand it, you have reported late to work at least 3 times in the last month. This seems to suggest that our policy is not being followed. Of course, this is not only a rule violation, it can be a real problem for others who work in the office and have to stay late or cover for people who are not showing up on time. Is there something going on that I am not aware of?"*

Recipient: "Well actually there is. I was hoping to handle things by myself and keep this private, but the truth is my mother was recently put in hospice care and it has been a very emotional and difficult time in our family. I didn't want to say anything, because I am not looking to offer excuses. I have come in late a few times; things are a bit more difficult with everything that is going on right now. I am sorry I let you down."

Response: "My goodness Chris, I am so sorry to hear about this. Please let me know if there is anything that I personally can do for you or your family. I am glad you shared this information so we have a better understanding about the situation. Is there something we can do with your schedule to help or do you need to take some personal time right now?

In the above example, there is a nurturing reply to offer assistance, including a gentle response regarding suggestions as to how you might help to address the situation. You want to be respectful and, in such a serious personal situation as described, as accommodating as possible within the limits you have available. However, the organizational issue remains—and others are impacted as well. Here you are offering the consideration of other solutions to this situation.

Step 8. Completing the Criticism Conversation

You have engaged all of the steps identified above and have determined the best response to the comments from the individual. Just as you want to have a clear plan for developing and delivering criticism, you want to have a clear plan to complete the criticism conversation. You likely have already considered what you believe would be a reasonable result. Depending on the totality of the conversation that now includes the dialogue between you and the recipient, you are positioned to conclude the discussion. The previous chapters have a number of considerations that should be addressed, including clarity in communicating your future-oriented expectations, your continued respectful manner, and your planned approach for follow-up.

Example: *"Hi Chris. It is good to see you. ... Chris, the reason I wanted to visit with you is to discuss the situation that has developed with the attendance policy. As I understand it, you have reported late to work at least 3 times in the last month. This seems to suggest that our policy is not being followed. Of course, this is not only a rule violation, it can be a real problem for others who work in the office and have to stay late or cover for people who are not showing up on time. Is there something going on that I am not aware of?"*

Recipient: "Well actually there is. I was hoping to handle things by myself and keep this private, but the truth is my mother was recently put in hospice care and it has been a very emotional and difficult time in our family. I didn't want to say anything, because I am not looking to offer excuses. I have come in late a few times; things are a bit more difficult with everything that is going on right now. I am sorry I let you down."

Response: "My goodness Chris, I am so sorry to hear about this. Please let me know if there is anything that I personally can do for you or your family. I am glad you shared this information so we have a better understanding about the situation. Is there something we can do with your schedule to help or do you need to take some personal time right now?

Recipient: "I appreciate your understanding. If I could adjust my shift for the next few weeks that would really help. I am sorry I didn't come to you sooner."

Now consider all that has happened. You have taken what could have been a very caustic situation and handled it with skill and sensitivity. You have correctly identified an issue, addressed it factually, offered an intermediate understanding, and engaged a dialogue by asking a well-developed question that gave the recipient the opportunity to provide additional information.

Imagine a different response to the same initial scenario. In the below example the facts are the same, the employee is dealing with the same difficult personal crisis with his loved one. The difference is the reaction and, ultimately, the result. Unfortunately this occurs all too often when others make assumptions, jump to conclusions, infer intentions, and work only from their limited perspective—without the opportunity to have a sincere dialogue. How would you describe the below example?

Example: *"Chris, I've called you in to explain that you are clearly violating our attendance policy by your constant late arrival. You apparently don't value your job or the others who work here. There is no excuse for this behavior and I don't want to hear any. You can either get here on time or start looking for another job."*

This is definitely a more efficient communication. I doubt, however, that you would consider it to be more effective in developing your leadership credibility. This approach violates the principles we have been discussing. In the first sentence the word choice is pejorative at best. The second sentence is nothing but inference and assumption and the third sentence circumvents any consideration of a meaningful dialogue—it's all monologue here. This is "it's my way or the highway" thinking. Which route do you want to take? Which boss do you want to be? Which boss do you want to work for?

Following these general steps in the conversation can help you to develop greater confidence in handling criticism. Of course, this 'script' is like training wheels, it is designed to give you just enough help early on to get you comfortable and started on your way; you still have to develop the actual skill to be successful. If it seems a bit awkward to have everything broken down into individual steps, realize that this is not the ultimate result. It does *appear* to be much more complicated when everything is spelled-out in such detail; however, this is just a way for you to begin considering the process. (Have you ever *read* the instruction for your washing machine? If, so you would likely be paralyzed in your attempt to ever do laundry again!) The goal is for you to use these steps as you consider all of the previous ideas and advice on handling criticism. As your confidence and skill develops the distinctions of these steps and the formal components will fade to the background as your own style emerges.

As if criticism conversations are not challenging enough, consider the added difficulty that can arise when the potential recipient is a boss, peer, friend, or a relative, the stakes can be even higher. Fortunately, there are some special techniques that can help to smooth these rough situations. That is the subject of our next chapter.

Putting It All Together: The Criticism Conversation

Chapter 9
Special Criticism Considerations and Techniques

"Life teaches us to be less harsh with ourselves and with others." ~ *Goethe*

Chronic Critics
Hurt the Ones You Love
Bosses, Peers, Friends, and Relatives
Careful Criticism Questions
Question Categories
Criticism Communication Techniques and Strategies

There are a number of special circumstances, such as dealing with a chronic critic, criticism involving loved ones or relatives, and criticizing a boss or co-worker, that deserve particular attention. Additionally, there are several criticism techniques that can be used in these and other situations.

Chronic Critics

Like all things related in considering human behavior, the techniques of dealing more effectively with criticism will not always be successful, especially when dealing with emotionally immature individuals or those we might categorize as chronic critics. These are the people that take our openness to criticism and use it against us as a weapon to make themselves feel important, rather than as a tool to help others excel.

People who constantly criticize are often insecure and many attempt to enhance their own self-esteem by belittling and attacking others. In this case, the attempts to offer understanding and even partial agreement with anything the critic offers can result in escalation or re-inforcement of further criticism. If you offer even a tacit agreement or apology, this type of chronic critic will often reply with something like, "Well let me tell you what else you do that's wrong!" In this case, the assessment process becomes all the more critical.

"Maturity begins when we're content to feel we're right about something without feeling the necessity to prove someone else wrong."
~ Sydney J. Harris

Some chronic critics will use criticism to their advantage, playing a game of psychological gotcha. Those who are plagued with insecurity and self-doubt try to enhance their own egos by trying to diminish others. For this type of chronic critic, the usual rules do not apply. Of course, there is no benefit to engaging in an escalating confrontation with an ego-limited chronic complainer. If these critics see you getting flustered, they chalk it up as a win. Conversely, if you handle the criticism effectively, they may gain little satisfaction from the encounter and find their next mark elsewhere. Often the only real course, depending on the severity of the critic, is to calmly offer your response and move on or remove yourself from the situation. Prolonged discussion will likely not be fruitful and will not satisfy the underlying motivation of the caustic critic. For the truly objectionable and offensive critics, they must know that you are unwilling to tolerate abusive behavior, and in some circumstances the best response may be avoidance. It is a delicate balance to remain receptive to fair-minded criticism while discriminating that which is not. We will address that topic further in a later chapter.

Hurt the Ones You Love

Sometimes those closest to us seem to receive more criticism—and criticism of a less-than-constructive quality. Unfortunately, we may unwittingly take advantage of the close relationship because we know the person so well. As a result, we may unfairly employ our fault-finding magnifying glass. Because we have a connection to the person we may become less concerned with tact, diplomacy, or courtesy; and our careful reflective process that we use before criticizing a stranger or co-worker is not considered to be as important. Of course, this is a mistake. We sometimes believe that we have carte blanche to "correct" those we love the most. However, this misguided approach can lead to resentment, hurt feelings, and emotional separation. Surely, those whom we know and love the most deserve at least the same consideration we offer to relative strangers before we offer criticism. Interestingly we seem to hurt the ones we love the most; because they love us, we do not expect them to change their feelings for us merely because we offer some "needed" criticism. A quick peek at the schedules of marriage counselors and divorce attorneys might suggest otherwise. The considerations for offering criticism to a spouse are no less important than when we offer criticism to an employee, student, artist, athlete, and so forth.

Perhaps of equal or greater importance is when offering criticism to our children—especially those who are very young and impressionable. Misguided correction and criticism spoken out of anger rather than reflection can leave psychological scars that can be difficult to heal. Remember the goal of offering productive criticism is to help someone grow, recover, improve, prosper, or excel. Keep this goal in mind. Make sure you are mindful of the power of criticism to either harm or help. When dealing with your children, as exasperated as you might become, the ultimate goal is to raise healthy, happy, competent, loving, and accepting children. The way you do that may require you to rethink your approach to giving criticism to those you love the most. The apostle Paul stressed the importance of providing gentle correction. The question is not whether parents should criticize their children, but how. The idea is to address what went wrong without causing them to feel terrible and crater their self-esteem. Perhaps saying something like, "You did this, it would be better if you didn't do that; we make mistakes, let's work on this so as not do it again in the future."

Before you offer criticism to a loved one, take a moment and examine your own heart. What is motivating you to offer this criticism? If it is anger or frustration, you may wish to wait until the emotionality subsides so that you can address the real issue that created those emotions in the first place (recall the Criticism Corridor). Before you criticize, consider what you want the outcome to be. In healthy relationships the goal is to strengthen the bonds that tie, not to bind them. Before you speak, try to ensure your words are well chosen and come from a compassionate, loving heart. Effectively providing criticism is not easy or efficient; and it can be all the more difficult when you are dealing with the extra emotional connections of those you know and love.

> *"Everything that irritates us about others can lead us to an understanding of ourselves."*
> ~ *Carl Jung*

Studies demonstrate that we often receive more criticism at home than at the workplace, although the criticism at home tends to be more sniping and is not perceived to be as potentially problematic because it involves someone with whom you have a relationship. However, these events can add up and have an adverse cumulative effect. Much of the home conflict could likely be better handled by giving greater attention to others and their circumstances, employing improved listening skills, and by disconnecting the auto-speak function we sometimes seem to have before we have carefully thought about our comments. Just as we want to do when delivering criticism formally in the workplace, criticism offered in the home should center on what you want to accomplish before, during, and after this event. In other words, do you want a productive and helpful discussion or are you consciously or subconsciously baiting an argument? Make sure you keep the desired end result in mind. It is always instructive to remind ourselves that our goal is to have a positive caring relationship, not seek conflict through correction.

Bosses, Peers, Friends, and Relatives

Clearly, dealing with individuals in the workplace can have a unique set of challenges. This is especially true when dealing with others who supervise you or who have no real obligation to listen. You will not always have the advantage of having positional power when it comes to dealing with bosses, co-workers, relatives, friends, and peers. As a result, a number of the techniques and tactics listed below can be particularly useful in these special cases.

"One key to effective problem-solving is asking the right questions." ~ R. Garner

---

Careful Criticism Questions

As indicated in previous chapters, effectively using questions is really one of the "secrets" of providing non-offensive feedback and criticism. This approach can be used regardless of the position or relationship one has to the potential recipient; it can be equally useful with a boss, a peer, a friend, or a relative. Frequently, we feel that we are required to have the "correct" answer to the problems or issues we have identified and spend little time with questions. However, questions allow us to communicate information as well as gain additional insight. When properly used, asking key questions allows us to get the recipient to more thoroughly consider their decision or position. A well articulated question allows you to communicate potentially critical information without making a declarative statement. Similar to the Socratic method of instruction, used skillfully, this technique can lead the recipient to come to their own conclusion regarding the topic. Questions allow you to provide information in a non-offensive manner that tends to short-circuit the natural defensiveness that many people experience when given more direct criticism. Instead of overtly offering directed criticism, you are merely asking questions that may lead the recipient to the conclusion that something may need attention.

Effectively using questions as a means of communicating information—especially critical information—is a skill that requires practice and preparation. When formulating your questions, think about the *quest* in your question! Where do you want to guide the person with your question? What do you want them to consider and think about? Questions develop people by helping them broaden their perspectives, allowing them to reflect on other viewpoints that have heretofore not been considered.

An important caveat, however, is to ensure that the tone of your question (as discussed in Chapter 4) is carefully monitored. If your question reflects an attitude of arrogance or your tone imparts a sense of condescension you have missed the point of this valuable technique. Additionally, negatively worded questions are not helpful. Although this may go without saying, using questions such as "Are you really that dumb?" "Is *that* the way we do things around here?" or "How could you be so thoughtless?" is not exactly what we're suggesting. The use of a carefully considered question in criticism-prone circumstances should be specifically designed to *avoid* eliciting defensiveness on the part of the recipient. If the manner in which the question is delivered is perceived to have an impression of superiority this approach will not be successful. Careful planning is critical.

Asking questions—rather than providing the answers—also requires you to listen attentively. Asking questions of others facilitates their active participation in the discussion and any subsequent decision-making process, thus likely increasing support and minimizing later resistance. Additionally, asking questions enhances the self-worth of others; they feel that their opinions count and will usually appreciate the opportunity to address issues that may potentially impact them. Questions not only allow for a more robust communication process, they afford you the opportunity to practice listening—demonstrating that you are genuinely interested in their comments and allowing you to gain information.

> *"I never learned anything talking. I only learn things when I ask questions."* ~ *Lou Holtz*

Criticism communicated by non-offensive questioning can be a good strategy for any of the groups of individuals we are likely to encounter. For example, assume a supervisor has decided to make a significant change in the way something is being done in an organization. Unfortunately, you realize that this different approach is likely to cause problems or delays that the supervisor has not adequately considered. You might say "That is absolutely not going to happen, it is a stupid idea, and you clearly did not think of the consequences." However, that is a pretty harsh criticism and you may not yet have all the facts as to what led to the decision or what other factors may be in play. As a result, a much better approach might be to use a few well-constructed questions, such as "That's an interesting idea, how do you think it might impact productivity?" "Have you talked to the boss about this idea yet?" or "What do the other supervisors think about this new approach?" The goal, as we have discussed with our new definition of criticism, is to help others to grow, recover, improve, prosper, or excel. By using non-offensive questioning you are able to guide the recipient to consider issues and perspectives that might have escaped attention—and all without once having to directly challenge the behavior of the individual.

Imagine the following dialogue with the above questions:

Q: "That's an interesting idea, how do you think it might impact productivity?"

A: "Well, I'm not sure; I was really focusing on the front end. I'd better look at that."

Q: "Have you talked to the boss about this idea yet?"

A: "No, do you think I should?"

Reply: "Well, it might not be a bad idea, just to make sure we are seeing the big picture."

Q: "What do the other supervisors think about this new approach?"

A: "I haven't really discussed it with anyone outside my area, but that's a good idea; I sure don't want to step on anyone's toes."

Q: "How do you think that schedule will impact Phil's involvement?"

A: "Wow, I forgot about that...I may need to give this a bit more thought."

Question Categories

There are at least three general categories of questions appropriate for our discussion: informational, consequence, and explicit (ICE). *Informational* questions can be used to both communicate and gather information. For example, "Could you clarify how this will...?" is a question that will not only yield information, but may cause the recipient to more carefully reflect on their decision. Similarly, questions such as "Can you give me a little more information on...?" or "How long have you been considering this?" are designed to both elicit information and solicit greater rumination on the part of the recipient.

Consequence questions provide the opportunity for the recipient to consider the outcome of their position or decision. For example, "What did the boss think of this idea?" "How will this decision affect the other units?" "What will we gain by taking this approach?" and "What are the risks involved in this tactic?" are examples of this consequence-reflective questioning. Again, the recipient may not have fully considered all options, and a question such as this may prompt that consideration.

Explicit questions are those that provide the recipient with an idea or a particular solution. Examples might include questions such as "What if we were to get the same result by doing...?" "What if we combined your idea with mine?" "Have you considered using...?" or "What if we were to instead do...?"

One form of question that can be problematic is the *"Why* did you...?" variety. Frequently when someone is overtly asked why they did something, the defensive shields are activated. *"Why"* questions are often accusatory in tone rather than our goal of non-offensiveness. It would likely be better to gain information with phrases such as "I am curious about..." "I was wondering about..." or "I am interested in your thought process in developing this solution."

Criticism via non-offensive questioning can be a great tool and may work especially well in circumstances where the criticism is directed at a boss, supervisor, or co-worker that may have positional power, but may not be considering the entire perspective. The boss may not take kindly to a subordinate offering criticism; in fact, it may have an unpleasant result especially if the boss is feeling threatened or defensive. Alternatively, few people would bristle if asked a few seemingly innocuous questions. Remember, it's the ultimate goal of helping others to grow, recover, improve, prosper, or excel that we must keep in mind; and there can be many paths to get there.

"And when you do find it necessary to criticize someone, put your criticism in the form of a question which the other fellow is practically sure to have to answer in a manner that he becomes his own critic."
~ John Wanamaker

Criticism Communication Techniques and Strategies

There are several techniques that may be helpful when dealing with criticism-prone situations, especially those that involve some of the special groups we discussed. These ideas and strategies were gleaned from thousands of surveys and hundreds of focus-group participants involving individuals from a variety of vocations and backgrounds.[1] These suggestions are born from the experiences of those who have demonstrated an ability to more effectively deal with criticism and are in positions where they must handle criticism-prone situations on a regular basis. Each approach may have strengths and weaknesses depending on the circumstance and your comfort level in using them. Criticism can be taxing for both the giver and the recipient; however, selective use of some of these approaches may help to reduce the tension. Additionally, research suggests if you think about and consider the impending situation in advance, then when confronted with the actual events it is much less stressful and your confidence is much improved. Mental rehearsal can be a very powerful technique and has been used in sports psychology for many years. One notable study[2] involved two groups of basketball players. One group practiced shooting free throws in the gym as usual, while the other group utilized visualization of shooting free throws in a classroom. After several days, the results suggested the group that mentally visualized and rehearsed their free-throw skills actually performed better than those who engaged in the actual behavior.

When dealing with criticism-prone situations, carefully considering and mentally rehearsing what you want to achieve and how you wish to accomplish your goal can be very helpful. Rather than starting cold, you will have already "experienced" the process in your mind's eye. This can have dramatic effects in easing tension and increasing your confidence level. Such a process affords you the opportunity to consider how to best communicate the criticism, evaluate what approach might work best for that specific recipient, and consider various options depending on how the situation develops.

"Explain as if the Other Doesn't Know" Technique

With this approach, you offer criticism in a similar style to that used in non-offensive questioning, though it is intentionally worded as if the person does not know the proper procedure or method—through no fault of their own. This can be a good criticism communication technique especially when dealing with co-workers. It allows you to communicate the information—in this case regarding how something needs to be done differently—without eliciting a defensive response. For example, you might offer criticism on how something needs to be done differently by saying something like, "You may not know this, however, we need to have…" or "No one probably mentioned this to you, …." Or "You may not be aware of this, however all of these need to be approved before they are sent out." Again, your tone and demeanor are critical. This approach can even work with perfect strangers. I was once leaving my office and noticed someone parking in a reserved spot. I could have said "Hey buddy, can't you read? You need to move your car!" That would have likely elicited a lot of defensiveness and an unnecessary confrontation. However, my approach was to say "Excuse me, you may not have noticed this, but you parked in a reserved space. I just wanted to let you know so you don't get a ticket or get your car towed. They are pretty strict about that around here." Instead of defensiveness, I was met with appreciation. Additionally, notice that my less definitive language allowed for other possibilities without increasing tension. For example, unbeknown to me, they may have had permission to park there.

Super-Ordinate Goal Technique

A super-ordinate goal is one that unites everyone in a group and requires cooperative effort. As evidence from the classic social psychology study conducted by Mustafer Sherif,[3] creating such a shared goal necessitates cooperative efforts and can override individual differences. This tactic focuses on the "we are all in this together" approach. It demonstrates to the recipient that we are all working toward some common achievement. A number of psychological studies have demonstrated that when individuals or groups recognize their efforts are necessary in order to achieve a common goal, there is greater cooperation. Even though individuals may have their own ideas about how something should be done, if they see their efforts as part of something bigger, cooperation is more likely. For example, if you are trying to get a group to focus on the big picture, you might say, "I know that we all have unique ideas; however, I am sure everyone understands that the ultimate goal is to..." or "There are a lot of individual problems that we are all facing; however if we stick together..." This approach can get people to think more broadly.

Use Appropriate Humor to Deflate Defensiveness

Careful use of humor can be another useful tool as long as it is not perceived as making fun of the person or making light of a serious issue—it can elevate the mood and may offer some perspective if a discussion seems to have been blown out of proportion. It is often a sign of a healthy ego and maturity to be able to laugh at our own folly. Humor can be tricky, however, as everyone's "sense of funny" is not the same. If you are in doubt about your ability to effectively use humor, it is likely better to use another approach.

Demonstration and Example

One of the best ways to communicate how to accomplish a task is through proper example. If someone is not performing up to expectations, demonstrating the right approach can be very helpful. This not only communicates that you are willing to lend a hand; it allows you to offer criticism in a manner that helps the recipient improve (G.R.I.P.E.). In many cases, you may not need to *say* anything, as your actions are your communication vehicle. Many years ago, I was a police sergeant responsible for a squad of five officers. As part of working the midnight shift, it was our responsibility to check our assigned police vehicles for proper fluid levels, including oil. Obviously, this is not a particularly glamorous task and it was often overlooked. One late night (actually early morning) I went into the squad room and asked if each of the officers had serviced their vehicles. Of course everyone indicated they had. I then asked them to step outside to my vehicle where I opened the trunk and handed each of them the oil dipsticks from their respective police cars, which I had removed earlier. Obviously they had not completed the required check and each knew they had been "caught." My approach, however, was to give them their dipsticks without comment and simply walk back into the police station. I never mentioned or spoke of this event again. This is truly a case where actions alone were instructive. Many of those officers later told me this was a powerful lesson, not just about that particular event, but in effective communication without words and in leadership. You can imagine that they consistently checked their vehicles from that point on—if for nothing else to make sure that I had not confiscated their dipstick again! Actions can be powerful.

Criticism Projection

Another technique that can be useful is to address the criticism as though it is a problem *you* are facing and ask the person—for whom it is really intended—to offer suggestions or advice on how to deal with it. This approach does require a bit more skill in order to not appear condescending or transparent; however, it is another tool in the chest that may prove handy. Consider a co-worker who seems to be out of sorts and is not working or performing up to their usual level. Rather than a direct confrontation about their slacking output, a disguised approach might involve saying something like, "I have really been feeling like I'm not able to keep up with everything these days; do you have any ideas that might help?" or "I seem to be on edge these days with all of the changes around here; what do you do to deal with all of this?" Interestingly, this approach may elicit information from the recipient commiserating about feeling the same way or about a personal crisis, health issue, or other external event that is impacting their life. Either way, the issue is being addressed and you may now have important information that allows you to view the decreased work output as a symptom of another circumstance. Alternatively, the person may say something like, "You know I've been feeling the same way, so I am considering starting an exercise program to get my energy up; you may want to think about doing something like that."

Another example might involve a fellow teacher who seems to be treating her co-workers and students with less respect and more abruptness. This problem has become noticeable throughout the school. Because the person is at the same level as you and the situation seems to already be at a tipping point, your approach must be carefully considered. Using this tactic, you might offer something like, "I seem to be feeling a little edgy these days and not being as respectful of others as I should be. I'm not sure what is going on but I know that it is not fair to others; do you have any thoughts on ways I can get myself back in sync?"

The goal is to have the recipient consider the situation that you have presented and offer some useful advice. As a result of this cognitive process and greater awareness to the issue, the anticipation is that the recipient will more closely attend to their own behavior and their own suggestions for change.

Expert or Third Party Involvement

On occasion the best way to address criticism most effectively is to allow another person to provide it. This can be especially true in close relationships or in circumstances when the potential recipient may not view you to be as objective as you would hope (or perhaps you may *not* be as objective due to the emotional clouding created by the relationship). For example, I had a friend who was a captain for a major airline, was an avid aviator, and was a fellow flight instructor. Despite this individual's superb flying and instructional skills his attempt to teach his son how to fly was less than successful. The scrutiny and criticism necessary to assist someone to master a complex skill such as flying an aircraft were viewed by his son as too personal and seemingly emotion-laden. In this case, the father's criticism of his son's emerging skills as a pilot did not work well. As a result, I was asked to step in to provide instruction (after I made sure the individual really wanted to learn and was not simply complying with the dad's idea). I was able to offer criticism in a more detached, less emotionally-laden way. My criticism was viewed by the recipient as needed instruction rather than a possible personal confrontation. Interestingly, he ended up not only excelling in his flying skills, joined the air force, became an officer, and went on to fly multimillion dollar jets! For this same reason, professional athletes seldom have their parents or spouses as their coach—too much potential for emotional confusion.

Getting expert input can be important for success. If we could go it alone, there would be far fewer psychologists, psychiatrists, and therapists. Lots of painful experiences have determined that "Therapy: The Home Version" is usually less successful and is likely to *contribute* to the problem. Sometimes it is best to get outside, expert advice.

Ask for Assistance

Asking for assistance with an issue is a great way to offer criticism to a boss, for example, who has provided you with an assignment that is overly difficult, complex, or vague. Rather than telling someone that they have poor communication skills or that their assignment was not clear, you may simply go to the person and ask for assistance. Requesting help is a positive. It does not raise the defensive shields of the recipient and it allows you to get clarification. As an example, assume that you have been given a task that requires much greater resources than are available—something the boss neglected to consider. You might choose to visit with the boss and offer something like, "I really need your help to sort this thing out..." "I'd appreciate it if I could get your ideas on something that would really help me out..." or "If you've got a minute, I would sure appreciate tapping your expertise to help me figure something out..." In each case you are not directly confronting the person about their lack of clarity or lack of consideration regarding the complexity of the task; you are merely requesting help. Many people are flattered when someone asks for their help; it is a compliment. When asked for assistance, people often feel a sense of reciprocal obligation to help. The end result: you provide the boss with a greater awareness of the issue and you collectively arrive at a workable solution.

Let the Facts and Stats Do the Talking

Another approach involves deferring to informative research and statistical data. If someone needs a little boost to get them thinking down a different path, the introduction of potentially more objective information can be very helpful. In this case, you do not necessarily offer direct criticism; you are simply providing some useful data that may suggest the prudence of a different course of action or needed change. This is an approach that I have used successfully many times. I once testified before a legislative committee about an issue where I could have been perceived as being overly critical of the committee itself and the legislature in general. However, my approach was to merely present facts, data, research reports, and official statistics that supported an important change in the law. In this case I didn't even offer a conclusion, I simply let the objective information do the talking. (By the way, the law was changed.)

Ask To Talk

Asking permission to talk with someone about an issue or offer a suggestion for improvement can be a particularly useful tactic in dealing with emotionally close individuals, peers, and co-workers. It demonstrates a sense of respect for the individual's time and position. For example, you might ask, "Can I speak with you about something?" or "Do you mind if I visit with you about...?" or "Do you have a minute to discuss something?" It is very likely you will get a somewhat automatic response such as "of course," "sure," "absolutely," or "you bet!" However, the person may actually be operating under a time crunch or have other priorities. If they indicate that now is not a good time, you simply say "No problem, would later this afternoon be OK?" or "I understand, how about around 2 o'clock?" Of course, this tactic is simply a way to "get you in the door"; you are now in a position to utilize your other criticism management skills to address the actual issue.

The Pancake Approach

As the old folk wisdom goes, "No matter how thin the pancake, it always has two sides." This is also true with most issues and arguments. In fact, this was one of the most cited suggestions or strategies that was offered in the focus groups.[4] Perhaps you find yourself dealing with your boss who has implemented a policy that just does not seem to be working. Rather than directly confronting the boss (and the uneven power position) with details of his failed decision, the pancake approach might be used. In this case you approach the boss, not to express your discontent for what is happening now, but to ask for his "perspective" on something you have been thinking about. You then begin a conversation that may start something like "The way I see things we are..." At this point, you begin to address the situation as you see it. You immediately then offer the "other side of the pancake" of the way things are going now—elaborating on any potential benefits—in order to call attention to the problems and a possible solution. You are not eliciting defensiveness; you are merely offering a different perspective for consideration. In fact, it is often useful to provide little further discussion after offering your pancake position, instead ending the conversation with something like "Well, I'm not really sure which is the best approach, but I thought this is something you might want to consider." Again, you are not directly confronting, you are simply presenting an alternative position for the boss's deliberation. Doing so does not automatically evoke the "right-wrong" mentality that can lead the boss to becoming defensive regarding one of his decisions.

These are simply a few specialized techniques that can be used when navigating through particularly challenging criticism-prone situations. You will have to decide which, if any, work for you and your personality. When used in the proper circumstance, such techniques can increase your chances of having a more constructive criticism dialogue.

We have now considered a lot of issues and suggestions related to giving criticism to others, including a step-by-step process and number of special circumstances. Now we will move to the other side of the criticism coin; *receiving* criticism from others. Of course, we must remain mindful of all of the many topics we have already discussed. The communication issues, psychological considerations, cognitive biases, and other areas we have addressed are equally important when we are the recipients of criticism.

Special Criticism Considerations and Techniques

Chapter 10
Receiving Criticism from Others

"To avoid criticism, do nothing, say nothing, be nothing." ~ *Elbert Hubbard*

> Criticism Generalization
> Criticism Professionals
> Criticism: Improving your Reception
> Effective Criticism Managers

Criticism is unavoidable. Period. No matter what your religious beliefs might be, it is clear that Jesus of Nazareth has been identified as one of the most influential leaders and teachers of all time. Though described as a person without sin, he too faced criticism regularly. He was criticized by his disciples who often did not understand him, he was criticized by religious leaders who thought only they were the truly righteous, and he was criticized by politicians who feared his message and impact. He faced the ultimate criticism; the criticism of the cross—where he was also criticized by one of the criminals who was crucified with him. If Jesus could not escape criticism, I don't think the rest of us have a chance. There simply is no behavior that is universally accepted; and some people seem predestined to criticize anything and everything. As mentioned previously, in conducting training sessions on criticism management for many years, I often challenge the audience to name any behavior that cannot be criticized. Of course, any answer usually meets with immediate criticism. We simply have to recognize that criticism is a part of life; however, we can manage the effects and impact that criticism has on our sense of self-worth.

Receiving criticism from someone who is practicing the principles outlined in the previous chapters would probably be much easier. After all, if the critic has followed all of the steps we've discussed, the recipient would likely be much more receptive, less defensive, and have a sense that the critic has their best interests in mind. Unfortunately, that is not usually the case. Many critics, especially those with positional power, have not given much thought to their delivery of criticism. Because of past influences and examples, we have been conditioned to believe that criticism should be caustic; some believe that it *must* be painful in order for it to *work*. Sadly such beliefs are misguided and counterproductive.

As a result, we must improve our criticism reception skills to balance the potential thoughtless delivery of less skilled critics. The aim is to rethink the issues surrounding criticism and work towards doing a better job of handling it. This will not be a perfect process and you will undoubtedly have challenging times when the situation may get the better of you. However, the goal is to put these ideas into practice so that you develop the skill of dealing with criticism more productively with fewer and fewer instances when the criticism of others overwhelms you. With time and patience we can all become more adept at handling the critical comments from others, recognizing the opportunities for improvement and growth that may be buried inside even the most acerbic criticism.

Criticism Generalization

It is easy to *say* that we have a choice in how we respond to criticism-prone situations. What is much more difficult is retraining ourselves and practicing the skills necessary to deal with these situations in a more effective way. As indicated previously, receiving criticism can actually trigger the flight-or-fight syndrome that remains from our early mammalian days. As you realize that you are being criticized you may feel your heart race a bit, your blood pressure rise, your mouth become a bit dry, and your skin temperature may change. If you feel particularly threatened by the criticism, you may even feel faint or lose peripheral vision. These sensations may cause you to become all the more focused on these manifest feelings, resulting in a recurring and spiraling cycle. You may feel a desire to withdraw (flight) or retaliate (fight); however, it may be best to simply realize that these are somewhat instinctual responses and succumbing to them may not best serve your long-term goals. In fact, focusing on these symptoms will likely interfere with your ability to accurately hear and assess the content of the criticism.

Unfortunately, this cycle plays out all too often in our interactions with others. Once we experience the association of these feelings with the criticism, we may begin to engage in what psychologists call response generalizations. Essentially, links between adverse feelings and events, circumstances, situations, or environmental cues are formed. These links can be so strong that we begin to suffer the consequences of the emotional reaction simply by recognizing the cues of a criticism-prone situation. The feelings and reactions that have been experienced in past times in which you have been criticized begin to emerge—even if the current criticism is being thoughtfully offered in a productive and constructive manner. This emotional linking can be like the feeling some of us may get when driving down the freeway and suddenly see a police car on the shoulder. Without additional thought, we may hit the brakes, as we experience that unsettled feeling—even if we are doing the speed limit. For some, this is a generalized pattern of response to the cue of the police car. When I was young, whenever my mother forcefully called out my full birth name—emphasizing every syllable and letter—I knew things were not good. I think I still get an emotional twinge if I hear anyone use my full name! In the same way, we may experience unsettled feelings when cued to the onset of criticism.

Similarly, when a child is summoned to the "Principal's Office" or an employee is asked to report to the "Boss's Office," this is frequently coupled with a not-so-good feeling as a result of previous associations with this setting. (These were the two most frequently cited remembrances by members in one study.) In the latter example, we must remember that people are reprimanded, scolded, suspended, and fired in the boss's office. As the employee heads to the encounter they may begin to experience anxiety, nervousness, or worry as they try to figure out what they might have done. In other words, they are experiencing a generalized pattern of emotional response to the events surrounding their summons to the boss. These linkages can be very strong and difficult to modify. As a boss, I made a conscious effort to change this association by asking employees to stop by the office for conversation and coffee. I also made sure that employee awards and recognitions were received in my office—all in an attempt to abate the negative associations that had been firmly established by my predecessor. Unfortunately, the generalized response to the office setting was firmly entrenched. I may have made a dent, but the patterns of emotional response remained. It was all the more difficult to extinguish as my office *was* the setting for occasional employee dismissals and formal reprimands.

Criticism Professionals

I doubt few of us would suggest that our day would not be complete without receiving a fair dose of critical comments from others—we typically would prefer to steer clear of criticism. One of the reasons we have difficulty with criticism is that we have not carefully considered how to best handle criticism and criticism-prone situations. We find ourselves floundering about, trying to evade the sting of criticism, but have not taken the time to formulate a criticism action plan.

There are, however, a number of people that are more experienced in handling criticism-prone situations, as their professions seem to be lightning rods for criticism. (I might add that many a building has been protected and saved by lightning rods!) As a result of this interaction of occupation and adaptability, some individuals are more skilled at dealing with criticism from others. Interviews with waiters and waitresses, for example, reveal they are constantly being criticized for service (getting seated, first greeting, making reservations), promptness (delivering menus, getting drinks and refills, getting the food to the table), food (taste, temperature, appearance), cleanliness (the table, the floor, the restrooms), and so forth. Notice, however, the wait staff is typically only responsible for a handful of these complaints—yet, as the most visible person, they must endure the brunt of the criticism. Further, some patrons believe that they are by far superior to the subservient wait staff—after all *they* are the customer—and may display the corresponding arrogant attitude and behavior.

One might question why anyone would put up with such criticism abuse and wonder how many of them can do it so well? Answer: Because if they do not handle the criticism well, they will not get paid (tips are their life-blood) and may even lose their job! I was recently at a restaurant where a man at the table across from me would clearly be classified as a chronic complainer. He was seemingly dissatisfied with everything. According to him the service was slow (it wasn't), the food served was not what he ordered (it was; I noticed because he had ordered the same item as me), and he wanted his drink to be refilled more promptly (apparently he believed that his tea should be replenished at the conclusion of each sip). To the remarkable credit of the waitress, she remained cool throughout. She had learned a valuable lesson of assessing the criticism for what it was—the ravings of a very unhappy individual—and did not accept it as a reflection of her own esteem or competence. When the grouch asked for a cup of coffee, he immediately complained that it was cold and undrinkable (this may have actually occurred before he tasted it—although in fairness, he may have had ESP). Without skipping a beat she immediately said, "You know, they just made a fresh pot, I'll be right back with a new cup for you." She didn't agree that the criticism was correct (it was not), she did not debate the issue (no sense arguing with a fool), and she did not quarrel (see previous parenthetical statement). She effectively managed the criticism.

Public servants are often in a position where criticism cannot be readily dismissed because of the responsibility of their position and their office. Success is found when they recognize that this situation can provide valuable practice in handling that unsolicited criticism, allowing them to become more effective criticism managers. One of the best ways to deal with such criticism is to focus on actively listening and maintaining respect for the critic and their point of view—deserved or not. Ultimately for the public servant, it does not matter if the criticism is valid or not, it is making sure that the criticism is *understood*. Typically, people just want to be heard and will often feel better about the situation if someone has listened with empathy.

We can learn from those who manage criticism regularly. Police officers, public servants, waitstaff, elected officials, complaint department attendants, administrators, and *many* other professions or positions require adept handling of criticism-prone situations. In addition, we can learn from years of research and study about better ways to deal with criticism from others. Of course, not all criticism is as ill conceived or as caustic as with our waitress. In fact, that is one of the crucial elements in managing criticism—to recognize when the criticism can actually be valuable and help you improve, even if poorly delivered. The goal is to *rethink* criticism in such a way that you become successful criticism managers.

"Get your friends to tell you your faults, or better still, welcome an enemy who will watch you keenly. What a blessing such an irritating critic will be to a wise man, what an intolerable nuisance to a fool."
~ Charles Spurgeon

Criticism: Improving Your Reception

In a study of private and public sector leaders it was found that the ability to effectively give and receive criticism was as important as any other aspect of the managerial function.[4] To more effectively address criticism it is important to become a skilled criticism manager. You must be responsible for how you assess and address criticism-prone situations and not view the events as a victim or as a bully. One who assumes the victim role tends to blame the situation, circumstance, and others. Rather than addressing the issue at hand, the victim sees the criticism as an unjust plot. The insecure bully reacts to criticism by escalating a confrontation. The threat of criticism is too much for the ego, so lashing out, blaming, and coercion are the tools of choice.

The criticism manager, on the other hand, may also feel the sting of criticism and feel a bit off balance; however, rather than ineffectively reacting, the criticism manager assesses the information, considers the possibilities, and thoughtfully responds to the situation. The criticism manager looks at the criticism as an opportunity—an opportunity for improvement and growth, a chance to learn about another's perception, to learn about what might have been done differently, to learn what motivates another to offer the criticism, and even to learn how to focus on remaining calm in a criticism-prone environment. The spotlight is on problem-solving, not confrontation. Keeping an attitude of respect—even in the face of unjust confrontation—can go a long way in defusing tense situations.

Those who handle criticism best understand that it is usually counterproductive to get caught up in the emotional outbursts of others. We do not want to get caught in the act-react cycle in which *reactive* responses, elicited by anger, irritation, or fear, erupt without careful thought. The criticism manager recognizes the importance of *responding*, which implies reflective consideration and choice. One of the best ways to think of the difference between reacting and responding is to consider the effects of a medicine that you have been prescribed by a doctor. If the doctor indicates that you are reacting to the medication, that is usually not good. Alternatively, if the doctor suggests that you are responding to the medication, that is a good sign. In examining those who display sound criticism management skills, a few general characteristics seem to emerge.

Effective Criticism Managers

1. See the Criticism as an Opportunity

This is a real hallmark of the successful criticism manager. The opportunity can come in many forms; it might be an opportunity to learn about yourself, your ability to handle tough situations, or to learn more about the critic. It may be a time to reflect, to grow, or to realize that the critic is not interested in helping you become better, only in their criticism. The Japanese character for the root word meaning criticism is the same as for opportunity. The effective criticism manager similarly considers criticism as an opportunity.

2. Recognize There May be Truth in the Criticism

Even if mostly inaccurate, recognizing that criticism can be a perception that others may share, it may be wise to consider it as a caution to re-examine your actions. It is always preferable to try to profit from criticism—see the potential for personal growth in the comments of others. Interestingly, sometimes our enemies may be more helpful than our friends. After all our friends are usually trying to be polite and spare us from information that might jeopardize the friendship. Our enemies, on the other hand, are not necessarily interested in being our friend or coddling our emotions—they will tell us things we might not necessarily *want* to hear but may *need* to hear.

3. Engage in Honest Assessment

It is important to be honest with yourself and recognize that the criticism—even if not well delivered—may still have a ring of truth. We must avoid ego-satisfying rationalizations, explanations, justifications, excuses, and counter attacks to alleviate the sting of potentially valuable criticism. Be discriminating in your assessment of the merits of the criticism. The ability to more effectively assess criticism is the main subject of the next chapter.

4. Separate the Criticism from the Critic

Although this can be difficult to do, the effective criticism manager distinguishes the criticism from the critic. Even if the critic is neither credible nor well intentioned, the information may still be useful. Focus on the lesson, not the teacher; the review, not the reviewer; content, not the container. Unfortunately, many psychological research studies conclude that this is a very difficult proposition. Even when people are coerced to offer a position to which they do not necessarily agree, those in the audience nearly automatically assume that one's external statements correspond with ones internal beliefs and attitudes. We psychologically attribute their criticism comments and critical behavior to their intentional desire to cause us harm; we infer their intentions based on their actions—accurate or not. Those who handle criticism well are able to better sort these distinctions.

5. See Criticism as Information

This is one of the real secrets of managing criticism. Information is just that, it may be correct or not. When another criticizes you, realize that it is not necessarily a matter of right and wrong, but may simply be a matter of differing opinions. When you look at criticism from this vantage point, you are less likely to fall into the emotionally spiraling act-react cycle. Just as the crew on the television series *Star Trek* was always able to communicate with other life forms from across the galaxies via their universal transla-tors—to better handle criticism we should consider it to be a word in need of universal translation, and that translation is "information." When you hear crit-icism, think *information*. When someone is offering criticism they are communicating information about the situation, about you, or about themselves. Recall that our revised definition of criticism intentionally includes the term "information" in its composition.

6. Psychologically Remain in the "Third Person"

When receiving criticism, don't get caught up in the rampant emotionality that may be whirling all around; instead look at the events as a dispassionate third party, merely observing the other person and assessing their tactics and motives. You want to be a witness not a victim. As a witness you simply ob-serve what is occurring rather than being an active participant—at least initially. Exercise your choice to not get emotionally drawn into the world of the crit-ic. It may be helpful to think of yourself as a detached scientist observing the interactions of an experiment. Alternatively, you may find it helpful to consider yourself to be a "just the facts" observer, reminis-cent of the old TV program *Dragnet*. Even though the comments may be pointedly directed at you, try to view them as a dispassionate third party that is at-tempting to assess the content, meaning, and intent of the information being presented.

7. Recognize the Potential for Personal Development

Look more carefully at how the criticism may help you—even if it is nothing more than an exercise on how to remain calm in the face of hostile criti-cism. Criticism is uncomfortable and you frequently have little choice but to hear it; however, if you are going to listen, you might as well determine what information might be there that could help you to better yourself. Challenge yourself to find *something* in the criticism that may help develop your character—even if that something is patience.

8. Do Not Dwell on the Criticism

This is often easier said than done. It seems to be human nature to focus on the negative. Some speakers and teachers will review their generally glowing participant evaluations but may disproportionately focus on the very few that may possess some destructive criticism. Ultimately we must learn that there is really no percentage in that approach. We know there are multitudes of reasons people offer criticism, and often the reason may have little to do with the recipient. Social psychology, in particular, demonstrates that we all tend to see the world not as *it* is, but as *we* are. If the criticism is accurate then 1) learn the lesson, 2) consider what needs to be done to improve, 3) implement the improvement, 4) get over it and move on! Life is too short to spin your wheels on some single episode of criticism. Get rid of the replay button; instead consider it a repair button that has fixed the problem—with no need for further attention.

9. Accept the Criticism if Correct: Learn the Lesson

Many research studies of management practices suggest that one of the best ways to learn—some would say the essential way—is through failure. Some have suggested that if we are not failing, we are either not learning or we are playing it safe, not striving to grow. As a result, it is inevitable that we will fail and be subject to criticism. When this happens, we need to embrace the criticism and examine the lesson that it provides. Although we often prefer to get out of a sticky situation quickly, there can be some benefit to making sure you have fully comprehended the lesson that is being taught. It is by far better to avail yourself of the correction of criticism and absorb the lesson *thoroughly* rather than *quickly*. If you move on too quickly, you may miss a great opportunity to improve or, worse, find yourself back in the same or a similar situation in the future. It is preferable to learn the lesson thoroughly once, so as not to have to repeat the "class."

10. Evaluate Improvement

The more you encounter criticism, the better you can become at managing it. Following the ideas in this book, you should see immediate growth, maturity, and improvement in the way you deal with criticism. That progress should improve with every encounter as you continue in your quests for personal and professional development. Expert criticism managers understand that recognizing their improvements in handling criticism more effectively is an important part of the personal and professional development. Some areas that you may wish to note as you consider your criticism management progress are listed below.

Signs of Progress in Handling Criticism
- Greater confidence
- Increased inner strength
- Active involvement—not being reluctant to address criticism-prone situations
- Greater commitment to effectively give and receive criticism

- Understanding that criticism does not equal accuracy
- Better ability to learn by managing the criticism
- Realizing that criticism is not as threatening as you might have first thought
- Seeing the humor in it; taking yourself less seriously
- Greater understanding of criticism and the impact it can have on other people

These are a few of the characteristics of effective criticism managers. As we will see in the next chapter, there are some specific techniques that can be used to hone this skill. We will learn that how we initially evaluate, appraise, and understand criticism is really the foundation for everything that follows; it is the crucial first step in learning to more effectively receive criticism from others.

Chapter 11
Assessing Criticism

"The trouble with most of us is that we would rather be ruined by praise than saved by criticism." ~ *Norman Vincent Peale*

The L.E.A.R.N. Method of Handling Criticism
  Listen Actively
  Evaluate the Criticism
  Acknowledge the Criticism
  Respond Effectively
  Navigate the Response and the Outcome

The L.E.A.R.N. Method of Handling Criticism

We've all heard the children's rhyme "Sticks and stones may break my bones, but words will never harm me." Of course, this childhood reply to the taunts of another is relative rubbish as it relates to the impact of criticism. In fact, recent studies clearly demonstrate that verbal abuse is by far more prevalent and harmful than physical abuse. Words have the ability to cut through us like a searing knife. Feelings of self-worth and an individual's sense of competence can be dramatically shaken by the words of others.

How do you reply when someone criticizes you? Do you react or respond? Do you seek vindication even before the critic has finished their statement? Do you retreat? Do you attack? Do you agree with the critic even if they are wrong? How do you handle seemingly hostile criticism? Become confused, angry, defensive, freeze, shut down, retaliate, withdraw, ignore it, laugh it off, internalize the anger, or go into a rage? Interestingly, criticism is a great opportunity to learn about *ourselves*. How we handle other stressful events in our life can be a proxy for how we deal with criticism. How you define success or failure, how accurately you can assess your strengths and weaknesses, and how you deal with your own internal self-talk are all indications of your internal capacity to handle general stress. The more effectively you are able to cope with the daily hassles of life, the more likely you will be effective at appraising criticism and not falling into the "it's either right or wrong" mentality.

"Our anger and annoyance are more detrimental to us than the things themselves which anger and annoy us."
~ Marcus Aurelius

When criticized, ask yourself: What can I learn about myself? How can I view this criticism as information rather than an attack? Is there a truth here that I need to hear, even if the criticism is hurtful? What fear or threat does the criticism bring up in me? Why am I taking the criticism personally? Interestingly, dealing with criticism can often follow the same general phases as when giving criticism. You must decide what you can do before getting criticized (e.g., seek guidance and feedback), during (e.g., keep emotions under control), and after (e.g., consider the outcome). Criticism can be like the painful sting of the physician's hypodermic needle containing valuable medicine; your decision is to determine if you will focus on the pain or focus on the gain.

Ultimately, if you can fog a mirror (you are alive) and do anything that impacts the circumstance of others, criticism is always possible; and some would say *likely*. However, when someone offers criticism it does not automatically render it correct or accurate. In reality, there may be many reasons that someone offers criticism and sometimes it has little to do with the actual actions of the recipient. As a result, one of the most important aspects of handling criticism is to *assess* the comments for content and accuracy. The real key to being an effective criticism manager is your skill in assessing the criticism. The L.E.A.R.N. method provides many of the elements that can help you in that appraisal process.

LISTEN Actively - *L.* E.A.R.N.

Often we get caught in the "reply trap" where we are so involved in crafting how we are going to respond to the criticism, we do not truly listen. Unless you carefully listen to everything the person is saying you will not be in the best position to assess the accuracy of the comments or gain clues as to the motivation of their message. Even if the criticism is not true, the one offering the criticism likely perceives it to be accurate. Try to refrain from responding too quickly. We listen more effectively when we are not defending. Oftentimes the critic may only need to feel as though they have been heard. They may even know the criticism is a bit exaggerated or unfocused, but they feel the need to comment. You will have to decide, once you have carefully listened, how best to proceed. Listen without defensiveness.

"Everyone should be quick to listen, slow to speak, and slow to become angry."
~ James 1:19 NIV

ACTIVELY LISTENING

Active listening is just that; *active*. It is not passively attending to information, it is actively engaging it. That is, listening for meaning, understanding, and with the intent to truly comprehend the critic's position. As indicated in Chapter 4, unless you fully concentrate on attending to the speaker and thoughtfully listen to their message you are not likely to be in a position to effectively respond. In fact, you could end up responding in a way that is completely off target.

Active listening takes effort and often involves interacting with the message and the messenger in order to truly understand the criticism. As discussed in Chapter 4, one of the best ways to focus on the *active* part in active listening is to ask questions. This helps in several ways. It likely allows you to get better information, it provides a natural pause from the conversation (especially if they are firing off their criticism like a defense attorney on pseudoephedrine), and it clearly demonstrates that you are listening, concerned, and really want to understand.

When you are listening to another you are usually formulating your own internal questions. For example, you may ask yourself "How did they come to that conclusion?" "I wonder why they think *that*?" "What information do they have that I do not?" "Why do they feel so strongly?" "I am curious as to where they got their information to arrive at that opinion?" or "How or why do they see things differently than I do?" (Alas, these questions are often accompanied by others of a more defensive and emotional variety that we will discuss below.) In order to be maximally effective, it can help to develop that curiosity and give voice to some of those questions when appropriate. For example, if a critic suggests that you are violating some rule or policy that you believe you are properly following, you might want to say something like "Can you tell me a little more about how you believe that the policy is being violated?" This allows you to get a better picture of how they see the situation and exactly how they are reaching their conclusion. You may need to ask a series of ever-narrowing questions in order to make sure you fully understand the critic's position. The criticism may be unfocused or imprecise, so you will need to get clarification on exactly what the critic is trying to communicate for you to properly assess the information.

Unfortunately, the usual response is often an emotion-based counteroffensive. It takes the proper active listening mindset and emotional control to secure the best results.

LISTENING MINDSET

When formulating your active-listening questions, it helps to have a *strategy* to employ in the way you are thinking about the criticism. Although hearing criticism can trigger the Criticism Corridor that was discussed in Chapter 5, having the right mindset can go a long way in increasing your criticism success. The goal here is to be *curious* rather than caustic. If you are able to *authentically* express inquisitiveness without conducting an inquisition, you will be more likely to get needed information and clarification without a commensurate increase in emotional tensions. If your questions come across as hostile or overly defensive, the likelihood of success is diminished. Try to approach the criticism with genuine curiosity as to how another might have arrived at their position (including that they could be right) and ask questions with the proper spirit of interest.

LISTENING EMOTIONS

Emotional reactions are always one of the biggest obstacles to effective communication, especially in criticism-prone situations. The emotional "noise" can hijack the understanding of the message. However, one of the positive byproducts of actively listening and asking questions with the proper mindset is that we often become less defensive. As a result of focusing on the information and understanding the critic's position, we are less prone to solely focus on our emotional response. When we are focused on formulating questions and asking questions for understanding we are short-circuiting some of the rather automatic defensiveness that often occurs when we hear criticism. Being aware of the elements involved in the Criticism Corridor (Chapter 5) can help you to anticipate and work to correct any potential adverse response.

EVALUATE The Criticism - L.*E*.A.R.N.
To evaluate means to examine something in order to judge its value, quality, or importance. We should not simply and unquestioningly accept the conclusions of others, we must assess received criticism and appraise its merits, potential, and applicability. In order to best evaluate criticism there are several important areas of consideration.

ENGAGE IN *HONEST* EVALUATION
It requires a great deal of personal integrity to honestly evaluate, assess, and appraise criticism. It is much easier to defend, deny, or attack the critic or the criticism. We must work past the potential emotional sting and determine if there is a ring of truth to the criticism. Even if the criticism is not well phrased or presented, there may be important information that we might be able to use to our benefit.

"If a man calls you a horse, pay him no mind. If two men call you a horse, look for hoof prints. If three men call you a horse, buy a saddle." ~Anonymous

---

Assessing Criticism

CONSIDER THE SOURCE

Social psychology in particular, informs us to the importance of source credibility.[1] Just because someone decides to offer criticism does not mean they are in a position that makes their comments valid. (Recall our waitress example.) In the process of assessing criticism you should ask yourself a few questions similar to these:

- "Is this person knowledgeable about the area they are criticizing?"
- "Is this person trustworthy?"
- "Is this a person who is trying to help me improve or are they being destructive?"
- "Is this person one who offered productive criticism to others or to me in the past, or are they a chronic critic?"

Psychological research tends to focus on two broad areas when assessing ones communication credibility, perceived expertise and trustworthiness (the first two questions identified above).[2] If the source of the criticism is highly credible, then that should heavily weigh into your assessment. This can be particularly true if it is criticism that you have heard before (psychologists call this a consistency phenomena). Conversely, if a critic is offering their uninformed opinion about a topic with which they are unfamiliar, the result of your assessment is apt to be quite different. However, it is important to honestly evaluate the source and not be too quick to dismiss the criticism. Although the chronic critic is motivated for reasons other than to help you improve, some individuals may offer useful information, even if you are unaware of their "credentials" to criticize. Regardless of the critic's motive, here we are concerned with *you*. It may be best to ask yourself, "Is there *anything* in the criticism—in spite of the delivery method or the deliverer—that could allow me to improve in some way?" If so, you may want to consider their criticism more carefully.

KEEP YOUR PERSPECTIVE

Even when criticism may be valid, it is important to not get "caught in the thick of thin things." In other words, the issue being criticized may be so trivial that the effort to institute change exceeds the potential benefit derived. Keep it in perspective! When evaluating the criticism how does it rank on the "Critical Scale?" Does it have life-changing importance or is it something less?

"When you swim in the ocean, you can be attacked by sharks and guppies; Don't worry about the guppies." ~ *Folk Wisdom*

TRY NOT TO REACT OR TAKE IT PERSONALLY

Okay, so this is often easier said than done; however, there is a big difference between reacting and responding. Reacting is part of the Act-React cycle, with little thought in between. *Responding* has the connotation of some reflection before answering. As mentioned before, consider thinking of it this way: If you go to the doctor and she tells you that you are "reacting" to the medication—that's usually not good; if you go to the doctor and are told you are "responding" to the medication—that's good news. It's the same in dealing with others; between the stimulus of the criticism and the response of your reply you have the opportunity to exercise a choice.

In considering your choice in criticism-prone situations, it is often best to resist the temptation to blast the critic, especially if the criticism is seemingly unwarranted or unjustified. Instead of lashing out, consider why this person may have this perception, consider if there is a grain of truth to the information—being very honest with yourself—or reflect on what this information is telling you about the critic; how *they* handle stress or other events. Both sides of the criticism coin are important.

There is a subtle balance involved in remaining open to the productive aspects of criticism, while ensuring that your own self-esteem remains intact.

Ask Yourself "What Can I Learn From this Criticism?"

This is frequently a very healthy attitude to take when dealing with someone offering you criticism. This approach also helps you to psychologically remain somewhat detached from the criticism. Instead of absorbing the criticism and potentially growing angry or frustrated, you are placing yourself in the position of an analyst. You are mentally assessing the information as a "third person" rather than taking each comment personally. This places you in a much stronger and more mature position in the criticism communication cycle. By converting your role as the receiver of criticism to an *observer* of the one who is offering the criticism, you place yourself in a position to better objectively assess the intention of the critic and the importance of the criticism.

As always, it is vital to recognize the opportunity for personal growth, either by accurately assessing the potential truth that may be lurking in the criticism, or by deciding you will maturely consider what you may learn from this encounter—even if it is the patience to deal with inaccurate criticism. You have the freedom to choose how you will respond. Don't be too quick to dismiss the criticism of others; you never know what potential growth opportunity you may find.

Accept that Criticism Can Be Unpleasant

In your evaluation of criticism, accept that criticism is inevitable and—properly communicated—can provide you with feedback that can help you to better yourself and your performance. That may not make receiving criticism more enjoyable, but if you are prepared with the proper mindset, you will be in a better position to consider the critical comments of others. If there is a lesson to be learned, be sure you fully embrace that experience. We sometimes wish to wiggle out of uncomfortable or unpleasant situations too soon—before we gain the insight we need to avoid problems in the future. It is far better to learn a lesson *well* than expediently.

If you are striving to reach new goals, it is likely that you will experience failure, setback, and complications. This is an opportunity to examine your mettle. If you simply are not capable of carefully assessing and responding to the criticism of others—using the techniques offered in this book and elsewhere—then it may be time for a cognitive shift—a change in thinking. You've got to be able to stand the heat if your goal is to be a firefighter. You've got to be able to handle criticism if your goal is to go beyond the status quo to become the best that you can.

"People ask you for criticism, but they only want praise." ~ W.S. Maugham

---

HAVE A SENSE OF HUMOR

A good sense of humor (also a term coined by early Greek philosophers) can help to diffuse hurtful criticism and help us to gracefully accept criticism that hits the mark. This does not mean that we flippantly laugh off the critical comments of others—that would defeat the potential gain in personal and professional growth. Instead, the ability to be amused rather than offended at the misguided comments of another can be invaluable. Similarly, the capacity to not take yourself too seriously and see the humor, even at your own expense, allows you to be more adaptable in managing criticism. In a study examining some of the important traits or characteristics of successful managers, Human Resource

Executives indicated that a strong sense of humor was a significant attribute.

Acknowledge The Criticism - l.e.**A**.r.n.
ACKNOWLEDGE THE CRITICISM

This does not mean that you necessarily agree with anything that has been communicated; it merely ensures that the critic recognizes that you received the comments. This acknowledgement may be nothing more than a brief statement such as "Thank you for sharing your thoughts with me about this, I appreciate you wanting to help." Alternately, your other options are often to withdraw, perhaps walking away without comment (not likely to be perceived as positive, especially if it's the boss offering the criticism), or immediately react. Unless you have had some practice, especially with the techniques like those offered in this book, you may wish to delay your ultimate response to the actual criticism (not the acknowledgment) so that you can adequately assess the comments and craft a reply. With practice, however, your ability to consider and appraise the criticism will dramatically improve.

RESPOND Effectively - l.e.a.**R**.n.

Responding to criticism is more thoroughly covered in the next chapter—this topic deserves its own space. However, how you respond to criticism is determined by a number of considerations, including all of the information identified in the L.E.A.R.N. model. You have actively listened, you are working to keep your emotions in check, you have evaluated the merits and you have started the response process by considering how you will acknowledge the criticism (not necessarily agree, just acknowledge).

The goal of your response is to effectively address the criticism without eliciting—in yourself or others—

increased tension or defensiveness. Sometimes merely thanking the critic for taking the time to visit with you and offer this feedback can be disarming. Remember the critic may be uncomfortable as well, so this tends to deflate the sails of conflict and put both participants in a "we're-all-in-this-together" frame. Unfortunately, the first response many of us feel is to immediately call attention to the minor inaccuracies in the comments or to look for ways to assert that we are correct and the critic is not. It is important to stay mindful of this impulse; focus on the information, assess it for content and look for the positive intent of the critic. Act as though they mean well, even if it seems that they do not.

"Why do you look at the speck of sawdust in your brother's eye and pay no attention to the plank in your own eye?"
~ Matthew 7:2-4

Additionally, as a part of your response, especially if the criticism is generally accurate, you may want to agree on a course of action that seems appropriate. If someone is offering a complaint, they obviously would like to see something done differently. Because we have converted criticism into information, we can realize that the critic is providing an opportunity to make things better (assuming the assessment of the criticism warrants such action). However, it is clearly important to get the other party to fully agree on the decided course of action and make sure there is no further miscommunication about what that action is to be. If not, you run the risk of having the critic later return with more criticism for the solution that was all wrong. Oftentimes asking the critic to provide a solution to the issue they have raised can be very constructive.

Assessing Criticism

NAVIGATE The Response and the Outcome
– L.E.A.R.N.

Navigate through all that has occurred during your assessment of the criticism and your response to the criticism. Once the initial encounter has concluded, consider what went well, consider what could have gone better, and consider how you could improve your criticism reception in the future. Delivering and receiving criticism is a process, not an event; and a good process must include an assessment of achievement. The L.E. A.R.N. method offers us the steps to better manage and assess criticism and allows us to engage in *"magnetism of criticism"*; turning what is seemingly a negative into a positive.

Ultimately, it's not just *knowing* these and other techniques to handle criticism; it is how you *apply* the information. After reading this book you may feel as though you know more about criticism and how to manage it than ever before; however, this will do little good if you do not actually place these ideas into practice. It is easy to read about how to handle something; however, the proof is in the action. The next chapter offers more concrete advice for dealing with the specifics of responding to criticism.

Chapter 12
The ABC of Criticism Management: Responding to the Critic

"In dealing with the critic, use soft words and strong arguments." ~ *Proverb*

> Ineffective Response Styles
> Effective Response Style
> ABC's of Criticism Management
> Dealing with the Caustic Critic
> Criticism Management in Practice
> Using the ABC's

In the previous chapters, we have discussed ways that you can become more effective in handling criticism. You have learned how to better appraise the criticism, glean the valuable information, and keep your emotions in check. The crucial activity of assessing the criticism as information serves as a foundation. This process is frequently not easy; people will inevitably fail and fall back into ineffective styles of dealing with criticism. While the goal is to always be a more effective criticism manager, the reality is that certain circumstances and events may get the better of you on occasion. Do not despair! Few people can quickly or easily make such a marked change in their life and in their ability to essentially reprogram their thinking about criticism. It takes a while and it takes a few failures; however, ultimately you will get it right more than not and benefit from the ability to more effectively manage criticism-prone situations. For example, consider that after working through the advice offered in this book, you begin to handle 50% of criticism situations better than in the past. That is an outstanding improvement! Although you do less well in the remaining instances, your improvement will continue. Your goal is improvement not perfection. (Those who can only accept perfection are likely those in need of therapy.)

Ineffective Response Styles

As previously indicated, the goal is to receive criticism through an evaluative process that allows you to extract useful information, use what is helpful, and properly categorize the rest. However, recall the problems associated with the Criticism Corridor discussed previously. Once we begin to feel the sting of criticism, we often start down the path of negative attributions, generated emotions, and potentially destructive or detrimental behavior. People will typically ineffectively respond to criticism in one of three general ways: with aggression, with passivity, or with passive-aggression. A brief mention of each of these might be helpful.

An *aggressive* response is really a counterattack that frequently results in a greater escalation of emotions. As indicated previously, receipt of criticism can cause us to R.O.A.R. (Retaliate, Offend, Attack or seek Revenge). This runs in opposition to everything we have discussed in better handling criticism. In reality, it demonstrates poor communication capability, poor adaptability, and immature coping skills. This is not the response of an individual who is practicing effective criticism management.

A *passive* response is likely no better. We may try to H.I.D.E. (Hide, Ignore, Dodge, or Evade) from the criticism or, even when the criticism is inaccurate and untrue, we may try to B.E.A.T. the criticism (Bear it, Endure it, Abide it, or Take it). Although it may not immediately escalate the situation, an individual who essentially surrenders at the first sign of conflict forfeits their ability to effectively manage or assess the criticism. In fact, some will quickly agree with a critic in order to escape even the onset of anxiety associated with the criticism. They will not truly hear the core of the criticism, will not be able to properly assess it, and will not be in a position to benefit from productive and constructive comments.

A *passive-aggressive* approach is equally unproductive. This too often stems from poor coping and communication skills. The passive-aggressive typically agrees with and may even apologize to the critic, even when they feel that they have committed no offense. Unfortunately, this can result in unresolved feelings of anxiety, frustration and, ultimately, aggression—especially the stealth variety. For example, there is the police officer who went into the Chief's office and told him all of the things she thought were going wrong with his leadership and the department. The Chief was taken aback, but was able to tell the officer that he "appreciated" her remarks. The officer was initially pleased with her performance, until she received her next duty assignment from the passive-aggressive chief: midnight shift...on foot patrol...in Mosquito Park.

Effective Response

Considering the process involved in the Criticism Corridor and by utilizing the criticism management techniques we have been discussing, our goal is to focus on effectively responding (versus reacting) to criticism, which suggests contemplation and assertive forethought. It is working to prevent the potential emotionality of a criticism-prone situation that can elicit a nonproductive counterattack. It is avoiding the impulse toward capitulation at the first sign of conflict. Effectively managing and responding to criticism employs all of the steps we have discussed. It is carefully listening to and assessing the criticism (of course, you are now thinking in terms of "information"); it allows you to extract the useful data, clear up misunderstandings, acknowledge what may be accurate about the criticism, and keep your self-esteem intact by ignoring the rest. Additionally, as mentioned elsewhere, regardless of your response option, it is likely a good practice to acknowledge the criticism. This does not mean you agree with the criticism, only that you have understood the critic. Without this basic acknowledgement the critic may believe that you have not heard them, that you are not being attentive, or you do not care. Merely acknowledging the critic can help to reduce a further escalation.

"A soft answer turns away wrath, but a harsh word stirs up anger." ~ *Proverbs (15:1)*

ABC's of Criticism Management
- **Accept**
- **Blanket**
- **Clarify**
- **Dismiss**

You've heard the criticism and, in keeping with the approach offered in this book, you have started to L.E.A.R.N. You've listened to the critic and the criticism, you've evaluated their comments, and you've appraised their merits; now what? When considering how to respond to the criticism, there are a few general methods that can be helpful, or what I call the *ABC's of Criticism Management*. (Actually it's *ABCD*...but that doesn't have quite the same ring!) After briefly addressing each element of the *ABC's*, I will offer a few examples.

Accept

Amazingly enough, as hard as we usually fight to consider otherwise, criticism can be accurate and ultimately helpful—even if poorly delivered. Of course, criticism that is delivered in the manner outlined in the previous chapters is all the better, as it is likely to be received without fully raising our defensive shields. If you have determined that the criticism is generally accurate, don't debate the "guppies" of the conversation unless you believe them to be critically important. You might offer something like, "You know, you are right, I could have handled that better; I appreciate your feedback. Thanks!" In this case a few things are happening. First, the critic hears that you are not disputing their view of your actions and—like most of us—appreciate your acknowledgement that you agree with their perceptions. This approach can also deflate tension, as there is no significant conflict between the criticism you've received and your own self-perception. Of course if you do not agree with all the critic has to offer, you may want to utilize the next approach—blanketing.

Blanketing

Blanketing criticism can best be considered by visualizing a blanket of fog that covers the criticism; some parts you see and agree with, other information is covered over. In this case you may choose to offer agreement with *part* of what the critic may offer. Perhaps you have assessed the criticism to be partially constructive; use that information for your own professional and personal growth and essentially ignore the rest. You may choose to respond by offering agreement with that which you have assessed to be productive and constructive; thank them for their feedback and simply do not comment on the remainder. You can offer emblematic agreement in one of three ways: with the criticism *in general*, with a *part* of their criticism, or as a *possibility*. The overall goal is to extract from the criticism that which helps you and your development as well as to reduce any tension, anxiety, or escalation. This approach can be very helpful in allowing you to acknowledge a part of the criticism that is accurate without erroneously accepting portions that are not.

You can also respond to criticism that is only moderately productive or useful by acknowledging that the information *may* be correct or has a *possibility* of being right. For example, assume that a co-worker has approached you and indicated that they believe that "your humorous style of delivery during presentations to the management team is demeaning and makes everyone look like our work is a joke." As you listen, evaluate, and assess these comments you know that you have received a great deal of praise from the management team *precisely* for your upbeat delivery, you always ensure you do not use offensive humor, you put the successful efforts of the workgroup in the spotlight, and you have doubts that others would agree with your co-workers assessment. Now you've got options; however, strangling is not one we wish to consider—at least not yet. You may simply choose to thank the co-worker for their comments and move on, even though that is really disingenuous as you really do not agree with anything that has been said. You might need to seek clarification (the next item) if you are unsure as to what the critic was specifically concerned about; although, given the nature of certain comments, this may be unnecessary.

One approach to addressing such criticism may be to blanket the criticism. Perhaps you might say something like "You know, you are right, not everyone appreciates

The ABC of Criticism Management

humor in the same way, and I'll certainly give that some thought. Thanks." Notice this statement has not agreed with the criticism at all, only with the general premise that there is a *possibility* that someone, *in general*, might look at humor differently. This type of response can keep emotions from escalating and tensions minimized. It allows you to graciously respond to the seemingly inaccurate criticism while keeping everyone's self-esteem intact. However, you will have to determine if this is the best approach in dealing with this individual over time. If the critic is generally a good guy and this criticism seems to be unusual and inconsistent, perhaps they are having a bad day and your polite response may be just the ticket. Alternatively, if the critic is likely to be fueled by this symbolic agreement—not realizing that you, in fact, have not fully agreed at all—then a different approach may be in order. Additionally, for a variety of reasons, you may need to be more direct in handling the criticism. If you are certain that you understand the criticism and have deemed it to be well off-target, you may need to carefully craft a response that addresses the misperceptions and facts involved. If not, you may be facing additional out-of-focus comments from this individual in the future.

There will be times, however, when you are truly unclear as to precisely what the critic is concerned with or specifically what they are criticizing. For example, if your friend comments that he just bought a vacuum and it "really sucks," I'm not sure if that is a good thing or a bad thing. I will need to seek clarity. In this case, you may want to use the "C" of our ABC's of Criticism Management, Clarify.

Clarify

In some cases the critic is not specific in their comments. As a result, you are not able to accurately assess the criticism and are unable to effectively reply. When this occurs, before you can effectively respond, you must seek clarification. This typically occurs as a part of our L.E.A.R.N. process. This requires your best active listening skills and assessment talents. You will likely need to be very directive in your approach, steering the critic away from general, pejorative terms and toward specifics. Ask the critic questions that use terms such as "exactly," "precisely," "specifically," or "in particular." The goal is to move the criticism from the abstract to the tangible. This may require you to ask for the specific behaviors they are suggesting that needs change. This is where the skillful use of well-developed questions can really help; both in seeking clarification and in keeping the emotional elements of the conversation in check. When presented with ambiguous criticism, you may what to ask questions such as "Can you tell me a little more about your thoughts on how this could be improved?" "Specifically what steps are you suggesting?" "Can you show me precisely how I can make this better?" The goal is to gain clarity. As an example, suppose a teacher criticizes your papers for being sloppy. What does that mean? Are they grammatically inaccurate? Are they poorly written? Are they missing needed information of which you are unaware? Are they formatted incorrectly? Sloppy can have many meanings and you will not be able to respond effectively until you determine precisely what the teacher considers sloppy when offering his criticism.

Of course, this is only an intermediate step; you will need to gain insight on the meaning of the criticism before you will be able to determine how you want to proceed — possibly acknowledging it if accurate or blanketing it if not. Some critics may have useful information that you can use to your advantage, however, they are not skillful in their communication. Seeking clarification may allow you to benefit from helpful criticism that you might have otherwise ignored if not for taking this extra step.

Dismiss

The last component of our ABC's of criticism response is "dismiss." Initially, there was some hesitation to include it in the response options because many people have a tendency to move too quickly to dismiss criticism. Because we usually have been conditioned to avoid criticism at every turn, dismissing the critic is a "quick-fix" solution that may seem to have some immediate appeal at the time. Unfortunately, when we reject criticism before we have honestly appraised its potential for helping us to G.R.I.P.E., we neglect a potentially valuable opportunity for growth. However, you will occasionally receive criticism that is simply inaccurate in all respects. Perhaps the critic has the wrong information, the wrong recipient, is emotionally venting, or is involved in some perceived ego struggle. In this case your appraisal process via the L.E.A.R.N. method may lead you to conclude that dismissing the criticism is the best course of action.

Though you have determined that the criticism is best disregarded, it is the *way* that you dismiss the criticism that can be important. Basically, your response will likely be determined by one of two general considerations: 1) the quality of the relationship that you may have or want to continue with the inaccurate critic, or 2) your assessment of the conflict potential or escalation factor that your response may elicit. For example, if the misguided critic is simply having an uncharacteristic bad day, you may say something like "Thanks for your input; I'll give it some thought." This can be a good way to shelve the content of the criticism without escalating conflict. On other occasions, it may be best to plainly indicate that you do not agree with the criticism. You might offer something along the lines of, "I appreciate your comment; however I am not sure that is the best course of action" or "I'm sorry but I do not agree with you assessment." Alternatively, depending on the situation, it may be best to say nothing (although it is *usually* a good practice to make sure the critic knows they were heard—if not, they may continue to repeat and reinforce their criticism, convinced that you did not attend to their comments). In yet another scenario, you may be dealing with a truly objectionable and caustic critic—the subject of the next section.

Dealing with the Caustic Critic
Despite your best efforts and intentions, some individuals are just chronic critics who can potentially become abusive complainers. When critics become overly emotional and angry, their potential for productive and constructive criticism is virtually nil. Although you may occasionally benefit from a spirited debate regarding criticism, there is no advantage to needlessly subjecting yourself to the abusive ranting of a chronic critic. Here are a few points you may want to consider in dealing with this difficult situation.

- Do not join in with those who shout, rant, rave, and so forth. It allows the critic to infer that they may have gotten the better of you.
- If the attack is in public, you might do something like raise your stop hand and motion them to accompany you to a more private place. Additionally, some have suggested using the individual's name with a rather firm tone, then immediately softening your voice to gain their attention.
- Redirect the individual's attention from anger by using constructive, repetitive verbal interventions:
  - "I can see how strongly you feel. Let's talk about this in another way."

- "I can see you are upset, I would like to really try to get the facts so we can address this."
- "I can see this is really important to you; please help me to better understand the real problem."
- If all else fails and the person refuses to de-escalate, you might say something like:
  - "I can't help until I can understand what's really going on and emotions are too high right now. When things settle down, I'll be glad to speak with you then." or
  - "I do not appreciate this behavior. When things are calmer we can talk again and I will try to help."
- Conduct a post-event assessment of the situation: What did the person say? Specifically what words were used and were they emotionally charged? How could things have been handled differently? What was your response and was it appropriate given the circumstance?
- Document the abusive or offensive behavior; if this is a part of a pattern or becomes one, you will want to have specific examples.

Criticism Management in Practice

Below are a few criticism-prone scenarios and possible responses. Of course, the limitations of the printed text require that certain assumptions are made. These are simply examples for you to consider as you work to become more proficient at criticism management. As mentioned in the preface of this book, anytime we move toward a new skill, there will be occasions when the techniques may seem forced, unnatural, or awkward. However, do not use these feelings as an excuse that will prevent you from really working on effectively changing your thinking and behavior. Use these examples as a guide as you continue your path towards becoming more effective at criticism management.

Using the ABC's

Relying on the ABC's of responding to criticism, an illustration is provided for how these techniques might be considered. Each component of the ABC's is identified, along with the assumption, a suggested response to the criticism, and an additional explanation regarding its use. (You may also want to look at the Responding to Criticism flowchart in Appendix B.) Keep in mind that you must do that which is most natural or comfortable for you. These are just examples; you will need to tailor the wording and delivery to something that best suits you—while striving for a productive and constructive result.

Accept (Acknowledge)

Criticism: "You are late again for the briefing and this makes us all look bad."

Assumption: It is accurate.

Response: "You're right, this is the second time I've been late in the last few months, I will solve the problem."

Epilogue: Offering an explanation may be appropriate, especially if the criticism seems to be overly general, possibly suggesting that the problem is a daily occurrence. However, this will only work to a point. You cannot be in a constant mode of excuses that do not ultimately fix the behavior.

Blanketing (Part)

Criticism: "You are late again as usual; you are *always* late to *everything*."

Assumption: You are late now, but you are obviously not always late to everything.

Response: "You're right, I am running about 5 minutes late tonight, there was a huge wreck on the freeway and traffic was at a crawl. Sorry."

Epilogue: You are merely agreeing with the part of the criticism that is accurate about being late tonight and the explanation is likely appropriate.

Blanketing (Possibility)

Criticism: "If you want to get ahead, you need to learn about everyone's job, be more social, and be willing to work late."

Assumption: There may be some slight merit to these comments, however, your evaluations have been outstanding—something the critic may not know.

Response: "You know, we could all probably do a little more."

Epilogue: You are just agreeing with the possibility that you could do more, not that you agree with the criticism.

Blanketing (In General)

Criticism: "You are not going to get promoted if you don't have better communication and presentation skills."

Assumption: You actually agree with the criticism—it's just not well targeted for you.

Response: "You are right, good communication skills are important in job success."

Epilogue: You are merely agreeing with the critic's statement, in general, not agreeing that it particularly pertains to you. If it seems appropriate, you might even follow-up with something like "Do you have any specific suggestions?" This changes the dynamic of the interaction and requires the critic to offer more than general criticism. Now they are asked for specific, constructive ideas.

Clarify

Criticism: "I don't think you are carrying your weight around here!"

Assumption: You have no idea what the critic specifically means by "carrying your weight" (assuming it is not related to your most recent diet).

Response: "When you say that I'm not carrying my weight, exactly what do you mean? What do you see that you think needs to be done differently?"

Epilogue: You may need to ask for clarification several times if the critic does not immediately offer specifics. Only after you understand precisely what the critic is concerned about will you be able to assess the criticism content.

These are just a quick sampling of a few scenarios in which the ABC's of Responding to Criticism can be used. Obviously your decision on which approach to take involves many factors; however, practice at addressing these types of situations is likely to pay dividends when the stakes are even higher. Even if it may seem awkward at first—try it, consider it, practice it. Only through such a process will you fully develop your criticism management skills.

Chapter 13
Seeking Criticism: Some Pain; Mostly Gain

"If you are hungry to grow, you will be eager to hear people's criticism." ~ Proverb

Seeking Criticism from Others
Criticism Seeking Strategies:
  Before Criticism Seeks You
Criticism Prevention Strategies

One of the reasons we have difficulty with criticism is that it may come at a time when we are most vulnerable and are not emotionally prepared. This can be especially true if we are involved in a project or activity that is already taxing our skills and capabilities. Criticism at this time can seem more harsh than intended and can catch us off guard. However, if you *invite* the productive criticism of respected individuals, you are better prepared to assess the information received. Because you are selecting the timing of the request and the particular critic, you are more likely to be receptive and open to the criticism. Actually seeking criticism from others can help you grow both personally and professionally. Rather than waiting for a crisis to develop (interestingly the root word for criticism is also the root word for crisis), preemptively seek criticism from respected individuals who you know will have your best interests in mind. On occasion I have been known to ask co-workers and others if they could suggest two things that I could do to improve. I may not always like or agree with what they say, but I always consider it valuable information, as I was the one who solicited the criticism specifically from them.

"King Solomon said, "Criticize a wise person...and he'll love you for it."
~ Proverbs (9:8)

Seeking Criticism from Others

Asking someone to criticize your work or efforts is probably one of the most mature yet potentially unsettling things we can do. It makes us vulnerable, yet, if properly handled, allows us to benefit from the wisdom of others. Requested criticism can potentially allow us to grow, recover, improve, prosper, or excel—the same goal as when we provide criticism to others. In a management study, respondents indicated their concerns in soliciting criticism from others; the results are summarized below:

What effect does *seeking* criticism have?
- It makes us vulnerable
- Allows others to point out our faults
- Gives others the power to evaluate our work when they may not have all the facts
- It makes us unsure of ourselves and become defensive
- It does not feel good to have others pick away at us or our efforts

Seeking criticism, of course, does not suggest that we should unquestionably accept the criticism of others (even though we have specifically asked them for their criticism), just as we would not naively accept unsolicited criticism. Not everyone is skilled in offering clear and helpful criticism in a way that allows us to use the information to our advantage. Some have not matured to this level and may be overly harsh or criticize the individual rather than the action. Unfortunately, it may take a few trial runs to determine who your best critics might be. Of course, it is best to attempt to avoid seeking criticism from those who knowingly lack the maturity to productively criticize, preferring to seek counsel from trusted individuals who have your best interests in mind (G.R.I.P.E.). However, don't avoid those who can provide you with an honest assessment, as that is what you really need to hear.

"We often stand in need of hearing what we know full well." ~ Walter Landor

---

Interestingly, some suggest that seeking criticism from less skilled critics *can* provide some potential benefit. For example, you may indeed get some valuable criticism from individuals in certain roles or positions even if the criticism is not skillfully delivered. If nothing else, even bad critics may allow you to work on your own skills at receiving criticism, ensuring you are focusing on the information rather than the emotion. Regardless of the proficiency of the critic, your goal is to seek and assess potentially valuable information that may help you personally and professionally.

Criticism Seeking Strategies: Before Criticism Seeks You

If you know you are dealing with difficult circumstances, do not wait for the crisis to develop. Preemptively strike at potential problems and pitfalls before they arise by seeking criticism that will allow you to perform better and prevent you from being blind-sided by criticism. Seek criticism before it seeks you. Some suggest that one of the best defenses to the sting of unsolicited criticism is a good offensive maneuver of seeking criticism often and early. Do not wait for things to spiral into a sea of criticism; consider your present circumstances and ask yourself, "Am I doing everything that I should?" "Do people feel they can tell me things without fear of consequence?" "Do I communicate to others that I value an honest assessment and do I make sure they know that?" "Do I actively seek feedback and criticism from others?"

"An individual's judgments can be no better than the information on which it is based."
~ Proverb

Seeking criticism can be a rocky proposition for some. The key is to seek and be open to the productive criticism of others without unnecessarily exposing your self-esteem to unwarranted distress. Finding the right individuals from whom to seek criticism and who you feel have your best interests and success at heart is the secret to success. The right critic does not mean someone who will offer faint praise or overly soften the criticism they offer. It is the person who can honestly and effectively tell you what you *need* to hear, even if you may not always *want* to hear it.

Criticism Prevention Strategies
In addition to seeking constructive and productive criticism, you can take steps to ensure you are not leaving yourself open for criticism that could have easily been prevented. Soliciting criticism from key individuals is important; however, you can go a long way in

limiting your "criticism exposure" by initiating a few prevention strategies.

Be Prepared and Organized

Ensuring that you are well prepared for your task or assignment can increase your confidence and minimize potential mistakes. Preparation includes fully understanding the requirements of the activity and possessing the skills necessary for a successful accomplishment. Organization implies that you have the requisite talent to plan and arrange the resources that may be needed to complete the task. Organization can be critical to one's success or failure. One recent study[4] suggested that there was a strong, positive correlation between organizing skills and organizational success. Those who are disorganized often flounder in their attempt to effectively plan or to even locate critical files or information. Some have suggested that they spend as much time trying to locate misplaced documents and materials as they do using the information once found. Obviously such an approach is ripe for criticism.

Do What You Say You Will Do: Live Up to Your Agreements

A key to effective management and leadership is to do what you say you will do. People will often ascribe greater positive leadership ratings to those who follow through on their promises. Keeping your word and developing a reputation as one that does so can minimize your criticism exposure. Interestingly, in doing leadership training for many years this issue is always at the top of the list in assessing one's credibility.

Be Aware of Strengths and Weaknesses

If we are honestly aware of our strengths and weaknesses we will be in a much better position to know what we can and cannot handle. Obviously venturing into a task or situation that exceeds our capacity is a sure invitation for criticism. However, personal and professional growth requires that we expand our limits and, thus, we will all experience times when our capabilities are taxed. We must recognize that these are the times we may feel the most vulnerable and may feel extra sensitive to criticism. Recognizing when we may need assistance or training to strengthen our abilities can help deflect unnecessary criticism.

Have A Handle on the Reality of Situations—Not the Sizzle

Sometimes we get caught up in the *idea* of some situation or circumstance only to realize that it is more illusion than reality. When we have committed to a task it is always best to be grounded in its authenticity rather than its hype. Those who focus on the "flash" rather than the facts may find their credibility flickering and their exposure increased to what would otherwise be preventable criticism.

Recognize Social Norms

Organizations and social environments operate within a set of expected patterns of behavior. Success in a particular organization may be contingent upon recognition and adherence to these normative influences. Those who choose to deviate from these accepted standards for behavior are more likely to be subject to preventable criticism.

Clarify Expectations

One of the most difficult problems occurs when there is a failure to effectively communicate the expectation of performance or outcome. If each party has a differing view of what an acceptable and successful result might be, a chasm of criticism can quickly develop.

We may not always like criticism, however, it is one of the best ways we can develop as individuals and as leaders. Seeking criticism allows us to develop and grow on *our* timetable rather than the schedule of others. It allows us to select the best time and place to receive critical information and then appraise and employ that which will help us to G.R.I.P.E. It communicates to others that we are concerned about our performance and want to solicit ways that we can improve. We may not always like it; but we always need it.

Seeking Criticism: Some Pain; Mostly Gain

Chapter 14
Critical Summary

"Let me never fall into the vulgar mistake of dreaming that I am persecuted whenever I am contradicted." ~ Ralph Waldo Emerson

Summing it All Up
Final Thoughts

Summing it All Up

As we draw this book to a close, we have taken quite a journey. We have examined the origins of "criticism," began a process of rethinking and redefining our understanding of criticism, and have considered ways that we might better give, receive, and seek criticism in our lives. We have moved from snipe to G.R.I.P.E. and looked at the benefits as well as the bothers in dealing with criticism. We have envisioned our new definition of criticism as a gift that we can offer to others and ourselves. Just as when reception on a TV or radio can be improved by adjusting the antenna for different channels, we can improve our reception of criticism by how we assess and interpret the information. The goal is to move from the pejorative words and feelings, and toward viewing the criticism as information that can be more objectively appraised for specifics that can help us to improve.

We have covered a lot of ground and considered many new ideas. Hopefully, we have come to view the communication of criticism in a much different manner.

By way of summary, below I have identified some of the key points that we have discussed in this book to better assist you in examining the big picture of better handling criticism.

G.R.I.P.E. Not Snipe

Sniping is a verbal attack and is most associated with the "old" definition of criticism. Our new characterization defines criticism as offering productive and constructive information intended to help others grow, recover, improve, prosper, or excel.

~~~~~~~~

Criticism: Appraisal, Assessment, Interpretation

It is not the words themselves that cause the greatest difficulty, it is the way we interpret and assess the information. Sometimes we give too much power to the critic instead of working to better appraise the critical comments.

~~~~~~~~

Why Do People Criticize?

People criticize for a variety of reasons, some of which have little to do with you. Others criticize because it is their job (coach, teacher, etc.). Criticism is an inescapable component of life. Better to consider ways to more effectively deal with criticism than to haphazardly allow it to adversely impact you life.

~~~~~~~~

Critical Responses

He can H.I.D.E. from criticism, we can R.O.A.R. as the result of criticism, we can try to B.E.A.T. the criticism, or—most effective—we can L.E.A.R.N. from it.

~~~~~~~~

Is it Better to Give or Receive?

It's actually both, but it is important to realize that once the critic releases their comments, the recipient has the latitude and the choice in how to assess and respond.

~~~~~~~~~

Critical Communications

The way information is communicated, especially criticism, can be as important, if not more important, than the actual content. Word choice, tone, inflection, eye contact, and many other components of communication can impact the effectiveness of a criticism communication. Active listening is one of the most necessary, yet under taught elements in the criticism process.

~~~~~~~~~

The Criticism Corridor

We often follow a somewhat predictable pattern when handling criticism. It is important to be sure we get the complete story (the Paul Harvey solution) and consider our own contributions in the criticism event.

~~~~~~~~~

Constructing Criticism: P.C. Criticism

Not political correct criticism, but productive and constructive criticism is the desired goal.

~~~~~~~~~

Before Giving Criticism

1. Consider your goal and motivation

2. Distill and identify the *real* problem

3. Focus on facts: Gather all the relevant information

4. Consider the time and place

5. Consider the psychological and emotional state of the giver and the recipient

6. Evaluate the criteria being used to validate the criticism

7. Visualize the encounter

8. Organize your thoughts

9. Send a clear message

10. Think win-win

~~~~~~~~~

Have the Proper Mindset
Having the right mindset or frame of reference when considering and offering criticism is crucial.

~~~~~~~~~

When Giving Criticism
1. Don't procrastinate

2. Maintain R-E-S-P-E-C-T (The Aretha Rule)

3. Be accountable and responsible

4. Remain calm – monitor your own emotions

5. Stick to the facts and be specific

6. Criticize the deed, not the doer

7. Make sure it's a dialogue

8. Be prepared for a variety of responses

9. Ensure effective communication has occurred

10. Focus on the future not the past

11. Be concrete regarding purpose and expectations

12. Acknowledge criticism occurs in context: It can be subjective

~~~~~~~~~

Critical Summary

After the Criticism

1. Be positive

2. Be accessible

3. Be patient

4. Follow-up

~~~~~~~~~

Putting it All Together: The Criticism Conversation

Consider the step-by-step approach to constructing a criticism conversation

~~~~~~~~~

Effective Criticism Managers

1. They see the criticism as an opportunity

2. Recognize that there may be truth in the criticism

3. Engage in honest assessment

4. Separate the criticism from the critic

5. See criticism as information

6. Psychologically able to remain in the third person

7. Recognize the potential for personal development

8. Does not dwell on the criticism

9. Accepts the criticism if correct: Learn the lesson

10. Evaluates Improvement

~~~~~~~~~

Assessing Criticism: The L.E.A.R.N. Method of Handling Criticism

Listen *Actively*
Evaluate *the Criticism*
Acknowledge *the Criticism*
Respond *Effectively*
Navigate *Your Response and the Outcome*

~~~~~~~~~

ABC's of Criticism Management

Accept – when accurate
Blanket – when partially correct
Clarify – when unclear
Dismiss – when completely inaccurate

Seeking Criticism: Some Pain; Mostly Gain

Seeking criticism can be one of the most mature activities you can undertake for personal and professional growth.

~~~~~~~~~

Final Thoughts

Criticism has clearly developed a negative connotation. When we think of criticism we typically think it must be negative. However, if we consider movie critics, literary critics, food critics, and the like, we can recognize that to criticize is to point out the *good* points as well as the bad in a situation or idea. To be a good critic is not simply to be negative. For example, think about the evaluations offered by a movie critic. Although they can certainly pan a film that they dislike, they also offer many positive critical evaluations of films that they may recommend. In fact, some people will wait for the positive criticism of the movie critic before deciding to see a particular film.

Of course, not all approaches in handling criticism will work well with every person. In fact, you will have the best success if you *first* work on better addressing criticism with those individuals who are a bit less challenging. It is often the case that when thinking of dealing with criticism, we go right to the worst case scenarios. This is not really fair to you or the process. If you want to develop better skill in handling criticism-prone situations, you've got to build your confidence in this communication process. Just as you would not take on a Black Belt on the first day of Karate class, you do not want to exclusively consider the biggest trouble-maker in your life as your first 'test case' in handling criticism more effectively.

How you handle criticism environments and the critics in them speaks volumes about you. In fact, much of what we talk about in better managing criticism is really more about you and how you want to be perceived in the world than about anyone else. Remember that people see the world as they are—from their potentially biased vantage point—not as it really is or even how you see things. As a result, there is ample room for misunderstandings. In fact, if you have handled criticism rather poorly in the past—either giving it or reactively receiving it—there will likely be some "adjustment time" before others will "trust" the change that you are attempting. However, once others realize that *you* have changed in how you view and approach criticism, and they recognize that this is not just some "how-to" fad, the whole environment can take a positive turn. When giving criticism, once people come to see you as a person that truly does have their best interests in mind, the interactions you have can change dramatically. Clearly, constructing more effective criticism using some of the techniques and suggestions offered in this book will likely have the best chance of success—especially as compared to the usual haphazard approach. However, though you may do a great job of crafting more effective criticism, you can't control all the varied aspects involved in every situation or every personality you encounter. It is important to recognize that even if the criticism you deliver is less successful than you might have hoped, if done well, with the proper spirit and intent, it will communicate to others the kind of person that *you* are. Success in handling criticism is not solely defined by the reactions and responses of others; it is more about the change that occurs inside of you.

If we focus on criticism as being improvement-oriented, we can transform our thinking in a way that allows us to view criticism as a teaching tool rather than a platform for mere correction. A conscious effort to avoid pejorative thinking and verbal attacks communicates a positive message to the recipient—building rapport and trust. When offering criticism to others, we must ensure it is with the intention to help another to grow, recover, improve, prosper, or excel; not because of a mere annoyance, inconvenience, or to fix blame. When criticism is offered with a caring spirit our own soul is nourished.

When we receive criticism we should strive to view it as information that needs our appraisal rather than an immediate affront to our self-esteem. Criticism sometimes provides such a shock to the system that we allow it to bypass our usual cognitive processes of assessment; however, if we view it as information, we can more easily subject it to scrutiny—not merely accept it at face value.

In the final analysis, we recognize that productive and constructive criticism is a sensitive and delicate undertaking. Before criticizing another we must examine our own hearts and minds, our own motivations. We must be mindful of the log in our own eye before we concern ourselves with the speck in the eye of another (Mt. 7:3). Ultimately what Peter tells us about Paul may tell us more about Peter than about Paul. We must be mindful that our criticism and correction of others is ultimately a reflection of our own spirit.

The best criticism comes from a caring heart and a sense to help others. If we are to criticize another it should be with the greatest regard for the other person, delivered with modesty, understanding, empathy, and generosity. Criticism *can* be a great gift for others and ourselves if we offer it with compassion, receive it with humility, and seek it with conviction.

Critical Summary

Appendix A

Criticism Action Plan
Write, Reflect, Revise

Before offering criticism ensure you fully understand your motive for giving criticism, what you want to say, how you want to say it most effectively, what "yardstick" you are using, and how you will follow-up to ensure success. Consider the following checklist as a tool to help develop your thoughts.

1. What is the Issue / Problem as I see it?

_____

_____

2. Is this THE problem? Is it a symptom?

_____

_____

3. What are your assumptions?

_____

_____

4. Is your information based on FACTS or conclusions?

_____

_____

5. What are the FACTS?

_____

_____

6. Where did you get your FACTS? (From Others?)

_____

_____

7. How does the problem or issue affect the work setting or situation?

_____

_____

8. What needs to be changed?

_____

_____

9. What will happen if I do not address the issue now?

_____

_____

10. What are the possible solutions?

_____

_____

11. How can I best approach this issue with THIS particular person?

_____

_____

12. What is the best time to address this issue with THIS person?

_____

_____

13. What action is necessary?

_____

_____

14. How can I best present this information?

_____

_____

15. What is the likely response I might anticipate from this approach?

_____

_____

16. How can I best follow-up for success?

_____

_____

17. What is my secondary plan if my initial criticism seems to be less effective than I had hoped?

_____

_____

Notes:

Appendix B

Responding to Criticism

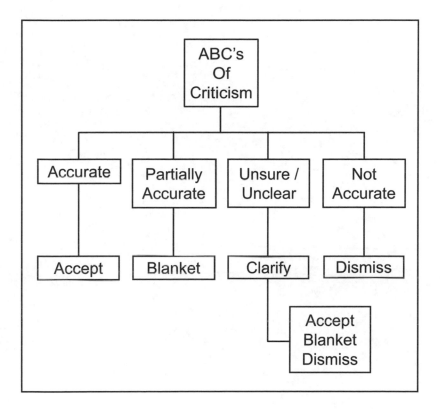

"Clarify" is only an interim step; you must then determine how best to respond.

Index

A

B

        Index

credible 53, 156
crisis 139, 191
criteria 79, 200
critic 15, 18, 21, 23, 24, 25, 26, 27, 29, 32, 33, 35, 36, 55, 73, 76, 104, 106, 126, 148, 152, 155, 156, 157, 161, 163, 164, 165, 167, 168, 171, 172, 175, 177, 179, 180, 181, 182, 183, 184, 187, 188, 189, 191, 192, 199, 201, 202
    caustic 23, 31, 175
    chronic 31, 32, 125, 126, 167, 184
    managing 27
criticism 125
    absence of 30
    after the 89, 103, 201
    as information 156, 162, 175, 197, 201
    at home 129
    before giving 69, 72, 78, 85, 89, 90, 199
    benefits of 21, 28, 29
    communication techniques 39, 125, 135
    constructive 14, 16, 24, 29, 32, 36, 71, 72, 79, 88, 95, 100, 103, 144, 184, 204
    destructive 15, 25, 101, 158
    dwell on the 158, 201
    effectively dealing with the 27
    give and take 31, 32
    give or receive 7, 31, 35, 199
    giving 8, 17, 18, 19, 31, 32, 33, 35, 36, 38, 85, 90, 93
    history of 11, 12
    importance of the 169
    manage 9, 173, 176
    management 10, 17, 18, 20, 38, 56, 143, 147, 153, 154, 159, 175, 176, 177, 178, 181, 185, 188, 198, 202
    manager 154, 155, 156, 163, 175
    managing the 36, 160
    prevention 189
    productive 128, 192
    professionals 147, 151
    question(s) 125, 130
    receiving 18, 20, 31, 32, 33, 35, 36, 38
    seeking 18, 20, 38, 189, 190, 191, 192, 195, 202
    seeking strategies 189, 191
    types of 21, 24

F

facial expressions 51
False Consensus Effect 49
feedback 14, 22, 24, 40, 76, 77, 99, 100, 105, 106, 130, 162, 169, 172, 179, 180, 192
filters 39, 48
flight-or-fight syndrome 149
follow-up 104, 105, 107, 187, 201, 207

G

gift 9, 23, 54, 89, 197, 205
giving 8, 17, 18, 19, 29, 31, 33, 35, 36, 40, 69, 77, 129
    criticism 9, 19, 25, 32, 33, 35, 36, 69, 70, 71, 72, 78, 88, 89, 90, 93, 107, 123, 128, 162, 199, 200, 207
goal 7, 8, 14, 16, 18, 22, 23, 24, 25, 31, 38, 69, 71, 72, 76, 79, 80, 81, 82, 85, 93, 96, 97, 99, 100, 103, 104, 105, 106, 128, 129, 134, 136, 137, 140, 148, 149, 153, 170, 171, 175, 176, 180, 182, 190, 191, 197, 199
G.R.I.P.E. in Action 11, 15
grow 7, 9, 14, 15, 16, 23, 27, 28, 38, 70, 72, 81, 89, 97, 103, 128, 132, 134, 148, 154, 155, 158, 159, 169, 170, 179, 183, 189, 190, 194, 195, 198, 202, 204

H

hearing 41, 54, 191
Help, Ask for 141
History of the Term 12
honest assessment 155, 201
humility 205
humor 106, 138, 160, 170, 180, 181
hurt the ones you love 125, 127

I

ICE 133
ignore 26, 162, 179
importance 70, 127, 128, 154, 169

improve 7, 10, 14, 15, 16, 23, 24, 25, 28, 37, 70, 72, 76, 80,
81, 97, 101, 103, 104, 128, 132, 134, 138, 148, 153, 158, 159,
167, 171, 173, 190, 195, 197, 198, 204
Improvement
    Evaluate 159
Ineffective Response Styles 175, 176
influence 25, 35, 38, 52, 103, 105
interpersonal distance 51, 53
interpret 17, 29, 54, 197
    criticism 17, 18

L

law enforcement 28
L.E.A.R.N. Method 163, 173, 183, 202
listen 36, 39, 53, 54, 81, 97, 129, 131, 158, 161, 163, 202
listener 42
listening 19, 53, 54, 55, 129, 131, 152, 164, 178
    active 54, 55, 98, 164

M

magnetism of criticism 173
management
    criticism 10, 17, 18, 20, 38, 56, 143, 147, 153, 159, 175, 176,
        178, 181, 185, 188, 198, 202
manager
    criticism 153, 154, 155, 156, 163, 175
mental rehearsal 135
message(s) 19, 28, 40, 41, 42, 43, 48, 51, 52, 53, 54, 71, 83,
84, 85, 88, 96, 98, 99, 163, 164, 200, 204
motivate 28, 37
motivation 8, 27, 29, 55, 72, 73, 126, 163, 199

N

noise 40, 41, 42
non-offensive 130, 132, 134, 136
nonverbal communication 51, 52, 53

O

opportunity 15, 21, 31, 40, 77, 107, 131, 133, 136, 154, 155, 159, 162, 168, 169, 170, 172, 183, 201
  criticism as 155

P

pancake approach 143, 144
passive response 176
peer(s) 129, 143
perceptions 24, 25, 179
permission
  ask 143
personal development 157, 201
phrase(s) 44, 45, 46, 49, 95, 134
phrasing 45, 46
place(s) 73, 76, 77, 79, 128, 169, 173, 184, 195, 199
police 42, 53, 71, 90, 138, 150, 153
policing 28
positive effects 88
power 18, 31, 35, 36, 128, 129, 134, 144, 148, 190
praise 12, 32, 77, 90, 106, 161, 180, 192
preconceptions 39, 48
preparation 35, 53, 71, 89, 130, 193
problem-focused 24
procrastinate 37, 90, 200
productive criticism 24, 30, 76, 79, 90, 128, 167, 189, 192
prosper 7, 14, 15, 16, 23, 28, 70, 72, 81, 97, 103, 128, 132, 134, 190, 198, 204
psychological state 199
public servant(s) 152, 153

Q

questioning 134
  non-offensive 132, 134, 136
questions 35, 104, 125, 130, 131, 132, 133, 134, 167, 182
  consequence 133
  explicit 134
  ICE 133
  informational 133

R

S